My Survivor Story

Chelsea Jackson, Kara Oakes, Tasha Rae,
Victoria Werner, Kathy Wilson

Copyright © 2022 by Lisa Nicole Publishing

All rights reserved. No part of this book may be used or reproduced by any means, graphic, electronic, or mechanical, including photocopying, recording, taping, or by any information storage retrieval system without the written permission of the authors except in the case of brief quotations embodied in critical articles and reviews.

The views expressed in this work are solely those of the authors and do not necessarily reflect the views of the publisher, and the publisher hereby disclaims any responsibility for them. In all cases, the names of individuals have been altered to protect their privacy.

Lisa Nicole Publishing
Gotha, FL 34734
www.lisanicolealexander.com

ISBN: 978-1-7375515-3-9

Printed in the United States of America

Note to the Reader

This book is compiled of personal stories from survivors that have experienced domestic violence. For some, this is the first time they are sharing their story. We celebrate their bravery.

Warning: This book contains specific details of abuse, suicide, rape, self-harm, and other sensitive topics. Please be advised.

Contents:

Chelsea Jackson 8

Kara Oakes..88

Tasha Rae..122

Victoria Werner...166

Kathy Wilson...213

Acknowledgments by the Authors

Chelsea Jackson

This chapter is dedicated with love and compassion to my younger self, to whom this chapter heals and frees, and to all other women who have experienced teen dating violence.

Kara Oakes

To Chad, for being my light at the end of the tunnel.
To my Winsor family for your unwavering support.
To Cecelia, who believed me.

Tasha Rae

To beautiful survivors, I hope my story can help you feel validated and heard. We are never alone in what we experience, no matter how much it can feel like it. You are worthy and were always worthy, just as you are. Share your story, speak your truth, and stand in your authenticity. The power in speaking your truth has the power to heal and protect future generations. I am proud of you, and I support you. No one can or will ever be you, and what a beautiful gift that is. Your empathetic soul is tremendously important in this world. You are a warrior, a teacher of wisdom, and a phoenix who will continue to rise.

To my parents, my brother, and my grandparents - You continue to support me and believe me, showing me I am capable and uplifting me in my darkest moments throughout my journey. I am so glad my younger self, the young girl who grew up knowing she could persevere and do anything she set her mind to, was surrounded by her family. Thank you for giving me the safety to heal, encouraging me, and protecting me. I love you all immensely. My dreams, no matter how big they seemed, were always supported, and I am blessed and grateful for that.

To the women I worked with in the psychology field, you always encouraged me to go after my goals and dreams. You supported me throughout my journey and continued to make me feel heard and seen. You will always have a place in my heart. I am so glad young women have you as mentors, leaders, and teachers. Thank you for being you and for the work you continue to do in advocating for mental health.

Victoria Werner

I'd like to dedicate my chapter to all the kind and amazing people who helped me along the way.
Jennifer, thank you for helping me when I was in need, guiding me to make the decision to leave him, sticking by my side, and creating a friendship I will cherish forever.

Kaylyn, without hesitation, you missed work to come to my first court hearing with me. Words can't describe how amazing you truly are. You have been my biggest supporter, and it means the world.
To my PACE girls: Thank you for being there through my entire journey and never giving up on me. The day you all donated money, so I could see a counselor made me realize that I am not alone. I can't thank you enough for everything. You all have a special place in my heart, and my friendships with you will never die.

Shout out to Stand Up Survivor for being the one and only organization to speak with me about domestic violence and for inviting me to your retreat. Even though you are states away, your organization reminds me daily that there are people wanting to help victims. I truly believe you are the reason I am standing here today, stronger than ever. The women who run this organization are angels, and I can't thank you enough.

Oddly enough, I'd like to thank all the non-supporters too. Without your negativity and your ability to put me on the sidelines, I would have never learned to put myself first. I would have never realized how resilient I am and how much of a badass I truly have become.

You made me recognize how many negative people I had in my life, pulling me down instead of building me up. Because of you, I now have an even closer group of great people in my life.

You all have given me a reason to live, a daily reminder to be the best version of myself and to always put myself first no matter what. I never understood my self-worth until now and my desire to help other women through their journey. I will make it my mission to grow from this, fight for what is right, educate others about domestic violence and open my arms to other women in need. Thank you.

Chelsea Rose Jackson

Facebook: Facebook.com/aboutchelsearose
Instagram: @aboutchelsearose
TikTok: @aboutchelsearose

About the Author

Chelsea Rose is a domestic violence survivor from Phoenix, Arizona. She is a poet, writer, and artist. Her experiences with domestic violence at a young age ultimately inspired her to be an advocate for others. From advocating for domestic violence and disability awareness, she has had the opportunity to attend two leadership conferences, one in Indiana and the other in California.

She hopes to grow stronger in her voice to help others in any situation- find their own confidence and be a voice for those who cannot speak for themselves. She is currently enrolled in Scottsdale Community College and working towards a business degree. In her free time, she enjoys writing, painting, and spending time outdoors with her fiancée and her pets.

The Art of Facing East

It was easy to hide the pain in my eyes when no one would make eye contact; until I locked eyes with the girl in the mirror. This wouldn't be my story if just one person had seen me.

I was 15 years old and in my freshman year of high school when I met my abuser. At 15 and in my first year of attending public school, I was a well-behaved child. I had no interest in dating at first, and I'll tell you why. Over the school years, starting in kindergarten, I noticed that I got crushes on girls instead of boys. In kindergarten, I "married" my best friend on the playground, and we celebrated with ice cream at her house after school. Her parents thought our relationship was adorable, but my parents took it a little harsher.

Growing up in a fundamentalist Christian household, liking girls was never an option, and they made that very clear. Therefore, after that talk, even though I was five years old, I kept what my parents said with me, and I veered away from dating altogether. As I got older, in middle school and junior high, I did not grow out of it; if anything, it got worse. I found *nothing* cute about boys but could make lists about why I thought girls were beautiful. In eighth grade, a boy asked me to the school dance. I turned him down because a cute girl in my piano class told me that the school dances were basic.

See, up until high school, I had attended private and charter schools. The school I spent the most time in, from first to sixth grade, was a strict private Lutheran school. I hated it there and begged my parents to put me in a public school. They compromised and put me in a charter school for 7th grade, then a different charter school for 8th grade. I was eager to learn and grow.

I didn't know what I wanted to be when I grew up, but I always got straight A's and was proud of my achievements. On my 8th-grade report card, my teacher described me as "smart, positive, and optimistic." I was one of those girls who looked myself straight in the eye in the mirror, pointed at myself, and said, "You are fabulous."

I always got complimented on my smile, so I knew my smile was my best feature. I had the confidence of a superstar and dressed like it. All of my outfits were bold and colorful.

Going into high school, my goals were to make friends and decide what career I wanted to work towards. I was very future-motivated with big dreams. My neighborhood best friend was a year younger than me and wasn't starting high school until the next year, so I didn't have any friends going into the new school. The first few days at the new school were intimidating, but I found a friend in my English class. We had assigned seats, and I ended up in the back, and she sat next to me.

I noticed drawings of cute big-eyed dinosaurs on the front of her binder, and we got to talking about art. I showed her my drawings that I had made of cartoon people. I loved to draw and color to express my creativity. I mostly drew people and focused on eyes and hands because I felt they portrayed the most emotion. She didn't look like my typical friends. She was more gothic and confident in her style. Her hair was black, had short, choppy layers, and was always straightened.

She drew small x's on the outside corners of her eyes with eyeliner and wore tight black shirts and ripped-up skinny jeans. I had never straightened my hair before and wasn't allowed to wear makeup. We had nothing style-wise in common, but we bonded over the drawings we passed back and forth during class. I was drawn to her uniqueness and confidence. Despite how much black she wore, she was cheery, social, and optimistic. Therefore, our personalities matched.

We quickly became friends, and she invited me to sit with her at lunch. She had several friends from different friend groups, and her friends would rotate what table they ate lunch at daily. We started eating lunch together every day, and shortly after, she introduced me to one of her friends, who turned out to be my abuser.

He was tall, skinny, and had short black hair. He wore a tan T-shirt with black skulls on it and baggy pants. On his pants were thin chains that connected belt loops. He smiled at me with a cheeky half smile. After she introduced us, she skipped away to another table to visit with some other friends.

We started talking, and I realized he wasn't as intimidating as he looked. He was the quiet kid who usually sat by himself in the back of classes. Even though multiple people were sitting at the lunch table, we sat at the end feeling almost separated from the rest of the group. It didn't take long for us to become friends. We talked about our classes and discovered that we were both taking theater and photography classes, just at different times.

We started sitting next to each other at lunch regularly, and even though we would talk to others in the group, we mostly just talked to each other. He didn't always have money for lunch, so I'd offer him my french fries or apples. He, my friend from English class, and I became a close-knit group. We started to hang out after school and on the weekends. We discovered that he and I lived in adjacent neighborhoods within walking distance, so we would meet up and then take a bus to her house.

It was a fight with my parents to let me start riding the city bus with my friends. Their parenting style was strict, but I had never broken their trust before, so eventually, they agreed. The conditions were that I had to check in with them every hour to let them know where I was and that I was okay.

Our favorite activity was going to the mall on the weekends to hang out. My parents would give me some money, and my friends would take me to Hot Topic, where they convinced me to buy black clothing or skull hair barrettes. My friend, the other girl in our trio, taught me how to straighten my hair. She also occasionally did my makeup, although I had to wipe it all off before I went home.

She lived with her grandmother and didn't have the best home situation. She had a rebellious spirit which led to her getting in trouble at home and school frequently. Her grandma confiscated her phone, and she was allowed out of the house less and less. I was allowed to stay the night at her house, but she was no longer allowed to hang out with us on weekends. Eventually, it turned into just him and me most weekends.

Shortly after that, in English, she passed me a note that said she thought he would ask me to be his girlfriend at lunch that day. I looked at her, confused because it was never brought up that he even liked me more than a friend. I panicked, and I don't think that was the reaction she was hoping for because she got confused. She scribbled fast on another paper and then passed it to me.

It said, are you going to say yes? I nervously jolted, "I don't know," and handed it back to her. She wrote back, "we'll talk after class."

I immediately got nervous. I had never had a boyfriend before, and I wasn't sure I wanted one! I tried to rationalize it in my head. He was nice, and we got along really well. We had known each other for a couple of months, which felt like a long time. I spent the rest of the class fixating on what I would do.

After class, I met up with her, and she walked me to my next class. I had one more class before lunch. She asked if I didn't like him or if he wasn't my type, which she explained was a shallow way to think. I told her I had never had a boyfriend before or even *kissed* a boy! Her eyes widened, and then she laughed. She told me that relationships were fun and nothing to be afraid of-- that I would even like them. She told me about all the boyfriends she's had but that she had never dated him because he was too quiet and withdrawn for her. The school bell rang, and she slowly went to her class, not caring about her tardiness.

At lunch that day, he did ask me to be his girlfriend, and I agreed. We told people we were together and were seen holding hands, but no one even looked twice. They didn't know who we were except for our group of lunch friends. My parents weren't thrilled when I told them I had a boyfriend, but they supported my decision because they trusted me.

They knew who he was because we were always spending time together. They thought he was odd but knew we were friends and had a lot in common. My 10-year-old sister didn't like him at all. She told me I shouldn't be his girlfriend, but I disregarded her because she was my little sister. My neighborhood friends supported me because they wanted me to be happy but they didn't really know him.

The first day we started dating, he kissed me. He could tell I was hesitant about it but was confident in what he was doing. I didn't mind the attention. He started holding me and running his fingers through my hair while we watched movies. I started to find comfort in his embrace even though I was initially timid about it. I became excited about our relationship. Our relationship grew stronger quickly, and I trusted him more and more as the days went on.

He wanted to get more physically intimate, but I told him I wasn't ready, and he respected it. We set clear boundaries regarding what I was and wasn't okay with. He liked to playfully push the boundaries, and some days he would get away with it more than others. About two weeks in, my hesitations about the relationship completely disappeared. It started to feel magical. I started finding cute things about him, like the way his hair curled in the front and the deepness of the brown in his eyes.

My parents started inviting him over for dinner, which was a big deal in my family. We all held hands and prayed over the food. My dad sat at the head of the table, and my mom sat on his right. My boyfriend sat to his left, and I was next to him. After a few meals with us, he started to say the prayers instead of my father. That meant a lot to my family and to me. We spent most of our time at my house and rarely at his.

When I asked him why he said it was because he thought his little brother was annoying. His mom was a single mother, and his little brother had autism. She tried her hardest to take care of the family but being a single working mother that fought breast cancer, she couldn't always provide adequate support.

After asking him enough times, he finally agreed to let me go to his house and meet his family. After school one day, we walked to his house instead of mine. His house was cluttered but organized, and most of the furniture was run down. The blue sofa in the living room was stained and torn at the seams, with indents in each cushion. The red floral patterned carpets were discolored and ripped at the edges but looked recently vacuumed.

Piles of papers and boxes were stacked outside the rooms on stands and shelves, along with antique knick-knacks. Stand-alone fans with broken blades stood in almost every corner of the rooms. The house smelled like cats which I thought was odd because they didn't have cats or pets at all because his mother didn't allow them.

His mom made us dinner that night. His brother talked through the whole dinner, listing fact after fact about sharks and dinosaurs. After dinner, we went to my boyfriend's room. We were not allowed the shut the door, but we could be alone there. His room was small and mostly just fit his twin-size bed and a long dresser. Dirty clothes were strewn all around the room. There were no decorations on his solid gray walls, just thumb tacks and pieces of tape where it looked like pictures used to hang.

I sat down on the corner of his bed, and he asked if he could show me his weapon collection. I was intrigued and wanted to see what he had. He sat down on the floor and opened the bottom drawer of his dresser. The first thing he pulled out was an old revolver. He laid it down on the bed and told me how it was passed down from his grandfather to his father and then to him.

He said he only had one bullet for it but was pretty sure it didn't work anymore. It was very special to him because his father left them when he was young. He said his mom let him keep it because it was an antique. Then he showed me three different colored butterfly knives. He flipped and twirled them around. I could tell he practiced and was impressed. He then pulled out two daggers, both old and rusty.

He explained that those were also antiques his mom bought him from an antique store. He then showed me a couple of pocket knives in different shapes and colors. The last thing he showed me was a pair of brass knuckles, telling me he got them from a store in the mall. I told him I liked his collection and wanted to get him a holographic knife for his birthday.

We sat on his bed and talked for an hour, but it was getting late, and my parents were going to pick me up. So, we went into the living room and watched his little brother play video games until my mother arrived.

At school, we became inseparable. We were always together between classes, during lunch, and before and after school. We passed notes to each other between classes all day long. He even talked to his school counselor about rearranging his schedule so he could be in the same classes as me.

My friend from English thought we were the cutest couple and took credit for bringing us together. We started gaining mutual friends from lunch, theater, and photography classes. One day before school, he gave me a matching couples necklace with our zodiac signs. We wore each other's zodiac signs and seldom took them off.

After we had the matching necklaces, things in our relationship started to shift. It started one Saturday when we were on the city bus going to the mall. There was a very skinny girl sitting across the bus from us. He pointed her out to me and whispered, "She's pretty." I looked at her and nodded in agreement. He continued, "You'd look that pretty if you were skinny too.

But I love you for you" I shrugged it off and tried to hold his hand, but he let go and crossed his arms.

I laid my head on his shoulder but noticed that he kept staring at the pretty girl. I was about 5 foot 3 inches and weighed 115 lbs. I didn't consider myself fat, but that comment made me start to doubt my appearance. The rest of the time at the mall was back to normal, but the comments got worse day after day.

At school, a popular girl came over to our lunch table to hand out flyers for a fundraiser the student council was putting on. When she walked away, he looked at me and said, "You'd look pretty like her if you were that skinny too, but I love you." That was the second comment he made about my weight, so I started reconsidering my appearance. The comments started getting more frequent and turned into, "You'd probably lose more weight if you didn't eat all that," commenting on my food at lunch.

I started giving him more and more of my lunch. What started out as me giving him some of my french fries and my apple turned into him eating my lunch and *him* giving *me* the apple. The food control continued even at my house as he would watch how much I ate at dinner.

I started to believe that I was actively trying to lose weight and that it wasn't coming from him. He played into it and would say, "Well, you shouldn't have that ice cream if you're trying to lose weight." I'd agree and put the ice cream away. I started to lose weight from not eating. I went down to 105 lbs. within a few weeks. At that point, I had made myself anorexic. I saw myself as fat every time I looked in the mirror and started calling myself fat out loud.

My boyfriend played completely innocent and started to get defensive but in a roundabout way, saying, " You're not fat, my love, but I support that you want to lose weight. But you shouldn't be so hard on yourself." At lunch at school, he started saying, "I know you're on a diet, and if you want to keep losing weight, you shouldn't eat that." Referring to the small number of french fries or apple slices I was eating. So, I went into the bathroom and made myself throw up.

Throwing up after eating became a regular habit until I was fully bulimic and couldn't eat without throwing up. Within another two weeks, I was down to 95 lbs. People started to notice my rapid weight loss, especially my parents. My face became extremely thin and narrow. I told everyone I had started a new vegan diet because I was protecting animals.

Everyone thought my answer was ridiculous, but they went along with it. My parents started making me vegan-friendly meals, which I would eat in front of them and then throw up after. My eating issues continued throughout the rest of the relationship and for years after.

One day at school, during my last class, I was so tired and dizzy from not eating that I had difficulty understanding the lesson. There was a test that Friday, so I wanted to make sure I understood and stayed after class to talk to the teacher. After school, I usually met my boyfriend in front of the library, and we walked home together. But I figured it would be fine if I didn't meet him that day. That night was the first time he hit me.

I remember that night the most out of everything. After I got home, I got a warm damp washcloth to lay on my forehead. I laid down on the couch in the living room while my mother was cleaning the kitchen. I remember the smell of bleach throughout the house. My mother always kept the house spotless. The smell was stronger in the living room, and all of the lights were on, but I chose to lay on the couch because I knew my boyfriend would be coming over soon.

He had called me after school and asked where I was and why I didn't wait for him. I explained that I wasn't feeling well and decided to go straight home. I told him I didn't want him to come over because I was sick, but he insisted and told me he would take care of me when he got to my house. Therefore, I agreed and waited for him.

As soon as he got to my house, he grabbed my hand gently and led me to my room. "It's darker and quieter in here," he explained. I walked to my bed to sit down, and he said, "wait..." He closed my bedroom door slightly then he grabbed both of my hands. He asked in a calm voice if I had cheated on him. I was very confused and explained that I had not and that I had to stay back to talk to the teacher about an assignment after class.

He tilted his head slightly and said, "Why are you lying to me?" I told him I wasn't lying and that he could ask my teacher. The conversation started to go in circles, his tone and facial expressions conveying his quickly rising anger. I tried to de-escalate the situation by reassuring him that I loved him, but it was like he didn't even hear me. I tried to hug him, and he pushed me away. I started to get frustrated because I didn't know what else to do.

In a final effort, I tried to change the subject, only to anger him further. He backed me into my waist-high dresser until I leaned back on it, almost sitting. He grabbed my face by the cheeks hard enough that my mouth slightly opened and said, "See, now I know you're lying because you're changing the subject." I tried to shake my head no, but he held it firm. He let go and slapped me across the face. In reaction, I grabbed my face and stared directly at him.

His mouth dropped open, and he looked stunned. He stood there frozen for a brief moment and then hugged me tightly. I didn't say anything but kept my hand on my face as if it was glued. He gradually held me tighter as the seconds turned into minutes. We stood there in silence. After a few minutes, he let go and took a few steps back. He put his hand over mine and moved my hand off of my face. He kissed my cheek and then my forehead.

He apologized, "I am so sorry, my love. I don't know what got into me. I have never hit anyone before." He pleaded, "Please, please, please, forgive me." He kissed me firmly and pulled me back into a tight hug. I told him that, of course, I forgave him; I was just shocked. He promised me that it would never happen again.

Of course, that was a lie, and I naively believed him. That would turn out to be the first of many lies. *Months later, I would find out he was the one that cheated on me that day.*

The next couple of days went better than ever. He bought me a stuffed teddy bear that I had been wanting and a promise ring. The promise ring was a thin silver band with a heart from Walmart, but it still meant the world to me. Additionally, continuing to shower me with gifts and knowing my love for the movie, The Nightmare Before Christmas, he handed me a coffin-shaped box that had a ring set inside. The top ring was small and was painted with a picture of Sally and roses. The bottom ring was larger and painted with a picture of Jack. Both rings said, "simply meant to be."

About a month later, I told my neighborhood friend about what had happened, and she disapproved of me forgiving him. I explained to her that it was an accident and that he didn't mean it. I showed her the promise ring and how he told me he would never hit me again. She didn't believe that he wasn't going to do it again and wanted me to break up with him. I told her that she didn't know him the way I did, which caused friction in our friendship.

She also didn't believe my weight loss was from my vegan diet. She told me she thought he was manipulating me and that I just couldn't see it.

I told my boyfriend that she had said she thought he was manipulating me. He seemed frustrated and told me he didn't think she was a good friend and I shouldn't hang out with her anymore. I told him that I wouldn't, but I still continued to see her. I kept both of them separate, hoping that they wouldn't notice. It worked for a couple of weeks until she noticed more and more bruises appearing on me.

After I told him what she said, he started hitting me again. Slapping turned into grabbing, shoving, choking, and biting. He could flip from loving and adoring to anger and rage so quickly that I started to feel exhausted from trying to keep up. Although, he always seemed to know the right sweet words to keep me close to him. I constantly had new bruises appearing all over my body.

More bruises were hidden than visible. I started telling everyone that I was clumsy, I fell a lot, which was true, but he was pushing me. Mostly everyone believed me because they thought I was anemic from not eating meat anymore.

I got creative with excuses, but my neighborhood friend didn't buy it. She was the only one who saw through what was happening, so I pushed her away.

I didn't leave him because I was convinced he still loved me. He constantly bought me presents and told me how much he loved me. He started telling me how beautiful I was again and how much he needed me. I felt important to him, and he continued to tell me he would stop. He didn't stop though, and it escalated into sexual abuse.

One night we were talking in my room at my house, and he started pushing boundaries. I told him I was uncomfortable and wanted him to stop. He started telling me how beautiful I was and continued until I felt guilty for not letting him. So, I sheepishly said okay. He asked, "are you sure?" His asking seemed odd to me because I wasn't sure, and he knew it.

When he started to touch me more and more, I got nervous. I told him I didn't want to anymore. He pushed my head into my mattress, tauntingly saying I had already told him he could, so he was going to take what was his. Afterward, he held me close like he always did, playing with my hair, telling me how much more he loved me and how happy I made him.

After he left, I took a shower and scrubbed myself until my skin turned red, trying to feel clean.

That moment opened the door for more sexual abuse as it became a regular activity. I told myself I wanted it and eventually started to believe that I did. I felt guilty, but sometimes it did seem like it was my fault, and I told myself, "Well, I did consent." Not thinking about how I only consented once and then changed my mind. All I saw was the love and attention it brought with it.

The attention he gave me though, changed too. He started mixing physical and sexual abuse. The physical abuse escalated into something I wouldn't wish on my worst enemy. I knew something was wrong but didn't know what to do or who to talk to. I was ashamed and scared.

I talked to him about my feelings about what was happening, and he started degrading me. He told me I was worthless and that no one but him would ever love me. He repeatedly told me I was only good for sex and that it would make my life easier if I just accepted that. I knew he was wrong, so I tried to break up with him. When I called him one night to do so, he said he would kill himself if I left him.

He took out his old revolver from his nightstand and spun the cylinder into the phone, saying he'd use it. I was terrified that he would kill himself and it would be my fault; therefore, I decided to stay.

I felt like I had no one to talk to because I had pushed away all my friends. I tried reaching out to my friend from English class, but she told me that I'd changed, and she took his side. I didn't feel comfortable talking to my parents about it, and I was too scared to talk to the school counselor. I didn't feel safe talking to my parents because I was afraid of the repercussions. I watched how they treated my older sister when she needed help, which wasn't reassuring. It felt like I only had him.

He still wrote me love notes and bought me presents, but they seemed empty because the next moment he would tell me I was fat and ugly. I started to slip into a deep depression that I called blue pains. It felt like cold pins and needles were constantly stabbing my veins at all times because of how much pressure and stress I was carrying. I started writing suicidal poetry to express myself and even thought about attempting suicide.

"You look different," my math teacher told me one day after class. "I know. I feel different." I responded. "Is everything okay?" She asked. I explained that I was trying to break up with my boyfriend, but he wouldn't let me. She let out a loud breath and said, "I'm so glad I'm not your age anymore. It'll get better as you get older, hun." Disregarding her, I went to my next class.

I had a black journal that I kept my writing in, and I always had it in my backpack. That same day in my Spanish class, the physical and mental pain became so overwhelming that I decided to ask for help but didn't know how. I started talking to the girl who sat next to me about the abuse, and I gave her my journal to read.

The first page was an analogy about how people were like clay. We mold ourselves into beautiful and unique pieces of art based on our surroundings and experiences. I felt like I had just started to mold myself into something before he took my piece of clay and closed it into his fist, leaving a replica of his handprint. I was terrified I would never be able to reshape myself into what I used to be.

Without getting any further, she said good writer and gave it back. I don't think she knew how to handle the situation.

Part of me wished she had shown concern and talked to the teacher about it or pushed me to talk to the teacher. I didn't need that big of a push; I was already looking for help. I just needed support.

After school, I was home alone because my boyfriend had a doctor's appointment, and my parents took my little sister out. I didn't know any other way out, so I planned to hang myself with a belt. I sat on my bed, cried for a long time, and then found a belt in my closet. I was standing by my doorway with it in my hands when I heard the front door open, and my little sister came running into the house, calling my name.

She ran down the hall and saw me standing in my doorway, crying. I grabbed her and hugged her so tight. She asked why I was crying and handed me a lollipop she had been sucking on. I laughed, gave it back to her, and told her I was just sad. She wiped my tears away and said, " I'm sorry you're sad, I'll make the sad go away." She went to her room and brought me back her favorite stuffed teddy bear.

I decided at that moment that I couldn't kill myself, and she was what I was living for. I told her years later that she had saved my life that day.

With suicide out of the picture and the abuse becoming more intense, I finally decided to talk to the school counselor.

I was nervous when I signed up to speak with her and created a plan to not say enough to where she would alert my parents but enough to tell her I needed help. I didn't trust her, so I wanted to start lightly before telling her precisely what was happening. When I went to see her, I sat down on the chair across from her, and she asked what was going on.

I told her that I felt pressured by my boyfriend into having sex. She went on to explain that boys our age have new developing hormones that they don't know what to do with and sometimes act on them in ways that girls don't understand. She ended the story with "boys are boys." Nothing she said helped me trust her enough to open up to her in any way, so I thanked her for the meeting and left her office.

Her dismissal of the seriousness of the conversation made me feel helpless and that I had no support from the adult that was there to help me. I felt that if she wouldn't help me, maybe I was being dramatic, and maybe I was the problem. After school, I met my boyfriend in front of the library as usual, and he looked upset.

I felt every nerve in my body turn "blue." He grabbed my hand tightly, and we started walking home. It was quiet between us the whole way home, but he never loosened his grasp. As soon as we got to my house, we went into my bedroom, and he pulled me to the corner of my room. He sat down on the floor and pulled me down as well. "I talked with the counselor today," he told me. My heart sunk into my chest. "Yeah?" I asked. "She said you went to her and told her I was pressuring you? Why would you do that? I never force you to do anything you don't want to do. Why would you do that?" He repeated the question multiple times, deepening his tone and becoming sterner.

I looked away because I didn't know how to answer. He grabbed my face to look at him, squishing my cheeks the way he always did. I told him I was sorry, and I didn't know why I did. He pulled me into his lap, sitting inside his legs, and pulled a little white box that looked like a first aid kit out of his pocket.

He opened it, and inside was a little black pocket knife that I hadn't seen before, a tube of Neosporin, some Band-Aids, and wet wipes. He pulled the knife out and opened it. He put it in my right hand and placed his hand over mine.

With his other hand, he grabbed my left wrist and flipped it upward. Hand over hand, he pushed the knife I was holding into my skin, making two cuts. I gasped as the skin opened and started to bleed. "Shh, Shh, Shhh," he said. "Feel all of the pain that you are holding on the inside become physical. Watch the blood that holds frustration leave your body. Just watch and feel." The cuts weren't deep but left two little raised scars on my wrist.

After a couple of minutes of watching it bleed, the pain did lessen. He opened a wet wipe from the white box and cleaned my arm and the knife. "Always keep yourself clean and the knife," he said. He applied Neosporin to the cuts, then Band-Aids. "Here, this is yours now," he said. He put everything back in the box, closed it, and handed it to me. He explained to me that he had first started self-harming two years ago in junior high, and it helped him cope with everyday stress. He stated that he felt like it was only right to show me the magic of cutting.

He kissed me on the cheek and said, "Now, when you feel overwhelmed, just do as I showed you, and if you ever try to get me in trouble again, I will kill myself and take you with me."

That's how my addiction to self-harm began. Even after this relationship, I struggled with it for ten years, to be exact.

I kept the box in my backpack to always have it near me when I needed it. I didn't continue to cut my wrists, though. I moved to my ankles because it was easier to hide. When I did wear shorts around the house, I told everyone I walked through the rose bushes to get to my friend's house, and they scraped me up. It would continuously happen because I continuously walked through the rose bushes.

Starting to self-harm didn't lessen the abuse any, though; it actually intensified because it now incorporated cutting me in various ways. I was terrified to reach out for help because he threatened to kill himself and me, and I absolutely believed him. I knew he was capable of terrible things. I coped for about a week by just self-harming, but then I decided the abuse needed to stop. I couldn't take it anymore.

I devised a plan to pretend to be pregnant. I told my boyfriend I was pregnant, and he could no longer physically abuse me because there was a baby inside of me. I also told him that sex would hurt the baby to get him to stop raping me. I put his hands on my stomach and said, "You have a baby in there" The abuse stopped immediately, and I thought I had won.

He started treating me gently again, just like he did in the beginning. I thought everything would go back to normal, but he became obsessed with the pretend baby. He asked if I was going to doctor appointments, so I told him yes, a friend's mom was taking me.

At school, while in the computer lab, I printed out a picture of an ultrasound and gave it to him. I had no idea what a three-week-old fetus looked like, so I printed the first picture of an ultrasound I found. It turned out to be an ultrasound of a woman who was six months pregnant, but we didn't know that. He folded up the printed picture and kept it in his wallet. He told me he felt like it was a little girl.

After school one day, we walked to the neighborhood park and sat on top of a bridge over a densely overgrown dirt canal. That became "our spot" to hang out. He held me and asked me what I wanted to name the baby. We went back and forth, suggesting girls' names such as Ella, Alivia, Talli, and Layla, but ultimately, he landed on Skylynn. From that moment forward, he only referred to the baby as Skylynn.

We didn't tell anyone about the "pregnancy" for fear of our parents finding out. While he was concerned for Skylynn and her safety, I felt like I could breathe. My bruises started to heal, and he wanted me to eat. I had to eat to feed Skylynn. I still had a habit of throwing up my food, but I was eating more overall. He even took me on dinner dates to restaurants within walking distance. My parents even noticed that I was smiling again and "had my happy back." I had no plan to tell him it was a lie or even a plan for nine months later when there was no baby, but I was surviving. Even the constant yeast infections and urinary tract infections subsided.

The peace lasted about a month before he started losing his temper again. He started hitting and sexually abusing me but would apologize to Skylynn afterward as if it was her he was hurting. I felt like he didn't care about me as a person anymore, and it didn't affect him that he was hurting me.

On the day I started my period that month, I had a new idea. After he pushed me down to the floor in the bathroom and spit on my face, out of anger, I told him that I had lost the baby. "Skylynn is dead!" I yelled at him. It was the first time I ever raised my voice to him. "You killed her!"

He didn't believe me, so I showed him the puddle of blood in my underwear. That was the worst night of abuse, too intense to describe here. His mom wasn't going to be home, and he was in charge of watching his little brother. I had called my mom and told her I was staying the night at my friend's house because it was Friday night, but the truth was he didn't let me leave.

The next morning when I woke up, he was still asleep. I snuck out of his house and went home. I didn't want to see him anymore. I wanted him completely out of my life. I felt so disgusting that I washed myself in the shower with bleach. My skin was burned and stung from the chemical, but it was nothing compared to what had been done to me.

I laid down in my bed in the dark room all day. I was afraid he would come to my house looking for me, but he didn't. I told my parents I wasn't feeling well, and they understood. I wasn't sure how I was going to tell him that Skylynn was never real, but I knew it was time to tell him. I was just afraid of the consequences.

I looked at myself in the mirror in my bedroom. It was the first time I had looked at myself in a long time. What I saw in the mirror scared me.

I used to see all the imperfections and pick my whole body apart. Now, I just saw a girl who was unhealthy, hurt, and broken.

She was covered in cuts and bruises, burns, and scars. She was not me. Her sunken-in, tired eyes watched me as I touched the markings left on her neck from being choked into unconsciousness. I touched my other hand to hers and cried as I felt her pain. She felt like she had lost everything in her fight for survival and was about to lose what little remained. She could feel the girl's chest caving in from pressure as she realized how far she had lost herself. Her light was buried so far deep it didn't even peer through the cracks.

As I lifted my hand away from the mirror, my tears became dense and heavy as it set in that she was me. I stared in the mirror for what seemed like hours, empathizing with this girl in the mirror until I finally decided to lay back down. I grabbed my little black journal and wrote a poem fueled by emotions,

> "Darkness creeps over; her dreams are hollow
>
> She's alone in this world full of pain and sorrow
>
> The pain is real; it will never go away
>
> The blood from her wrists is here to stay
>
> Nothing can fill the hole in her heart

It's there forever, 'forever do us part'

She's bleeding from the inside out

No one knows what it's all about

Pins and needles stab her veins

She cries and screams at the pain

Her thoughts surrender; there's no hope at all

Her heart gave in and took the fall

A slit down her wrist, A slit down her leg

But nothing will take the true pain away

She sits on her bed; her thoughts start to fade

She wishes to die; her decision is made

A glimpse of the razor shimmers in the light

She grips it again, only this time real tight

No one saw the pain held inside

Nobody knew her smile had lied

A stream of blood traced her arm to the floor

Then down her leg just like before

But this time was deeper, her escape from this hell

Her secrets were gone, never to tell

Her locks were broken, and the key was burned

>She ran from time; the clock was turned
>
>Suicide was the answer, the trophy to win
>
>Held to this world by guilt and sin
>
>A permanent solution; it's always the same
>
>It's the gift of life but the curse of the game."

I laid my pen down, closed my notebook, and went to bed.

The next day I was woken up by my mother screaming my name. I threw on a hoodie that covered all my markings and went to see what she needed. It was about one in the afternoon, and the house smelled like burnt popcorn. I walked down the hallway to the kitchen and saw my parents sitting at the dining room table, livid.

My father had his elbow on the table, holding his head, looking down. He didn't look up at me. My mom had her arms crossed but stood up as soon as I entered the room. "I just got a call from your boyfriend's mom," she said. My heart sank so deep I swear it fell on the floor.

I knew where this was going, and I couldn't stop it. It was my biggest fear for my parents to find out anything that had been happening. In their eyes, I was still the perfect, sinless girl.

My mom raised her voice into a yell and explained that their preacher told my boyfriend's mom that her son had lost a baby. She screamed, "LOST A BABY!" She became frantic as she continued, "You were pregnant?! You had sex?! Is that why you've been wearing these baggie jackets?! How could you not even tell us!!" She didn't even pause to let me get a word in, and my eyes filled with tears as I felt the final pieces of my world crumble.

"We trusted you! Have you seen any doctors?! Do you even understand how this feels finding this out from his mom and not you?!" she paused. My dad still didn't look up, but I could tell he was crying. My dad was my superhero, so making him cry felt horrible. I took a deep breath in and said, "I'm sorry. I really am. But the truth is, I was never pregnant. I pretended to be."

Now was the time for me to decide if I was going to admit to the abuse or continue to protect him. Still, to this day, I don't know why, but I chose to protect him. "WHY?!" She screamed. "I don't know why," is all I answered. In fear of repercussions, I felt pressured to stay silent about the abuse.

"His mom said he carved 'I'm sorry Skylynn into his leg!! And he even had a picture of an ultrasound! How messed up are you, Chelsea?!" my mom yelled. Again, all I could say was, " I don't know." "Well, that means you're having sex, though, right?? You're 15!! You knew not to have sex until you were married. We bought you a purity ring!!" she continued.

At this point, tears began streaming down my face. I felt guilty like I had let them down, and I felt pressured to have to lie. I explained how I told him he got me pregnant in other ways, but he believed me because he didn't know any better. They believed me but expressed frustration with my lies.

"So, you admit to messing around?! I'm so livid right now I can't look at you. Go to your room, and don't come out," she said firmly and sternly. I looked over at my dad, but he still hadn't moved and didn't look at me. I went to my room and closed the door.

I grabbed the white box, took out the pocket knife, and cut my leg so deep I could see the layers of fat. As soon as my skin opened that wide, I panicked. I didn't know what to do, so I grabbed a knee-length sock off of my floor and wrapped it tight around my ankle. It bled through my sock, but I had no other solution, so I left it.

I stayed in my room until dinner was done, and they called me to the table. They were still visibly mad, but they were done lashing out. We sat at the table and were silent until my sister was done eating, and she was excused to go play. Once it was just my parents and me, they explained their disappointment in me and how badly I had hurt them.

They told me that I could no longer have a 16th birthday party because I wasn't mature enough and that they scheduled an STD test that I had to do. Furthermore, I was no longer allowed to be dating my boyfriend, and they would monitor my every move to ensure I wasn't seeing him. That part was a blessing and a curse. It was the forced separation I needed from him. It only lasted a few weeks, and then my parents stopped monitoring me.

His mom also told him that Skylynn was never real. I was thankful I didn't have to do that, either. I got my cell phone taken away, so he couldn't call or text me anymore. I would have to wait to see him at school to break up with him in person. I was afraid that he would do something drastic at the school, but I felt safer there than alone with him.

As far as what my parents believed, there was no real reason for an STD test, but it came back negative, which I was grateful for. I was also grateful that I never did get pregnant from him because I was too young and broken to have the responsibility of his child. It was also made clear that abortion was never an option, even if conceived by rape.

When I went to school the next day, I met him outside the library like we usually did. His body language was guarded. I looked at the floor while I walked to him. As soon as I got near him, I said, "I'm sorry." I tried to make eye contact with him, but he looked away. He said, "This isn't over," and turned to walk away. I grabbed the sleeve of his jacket, and he turned back around to face me. "I'm not allowed to see you anymore. I'm breaking up with you for real," I told him.

His eyes widened, and I could hear his teeth grind. He didn't respond or blink. He held my gaze for a few moments in silence and then walked away. I had no idea what his lack of response meant, but I was positive that meant we were broken up. Most of our classes were near each other, so we saw each other in passing. Between my second and third classes, he passed me a note and kept walking.

I opened it and what I saw terrified me. He had written largely in blood, "As you wish." The paper behind it had a drawing of me, hanging from the balcony of the school library, naked, with the word "Whore" carved into my chest. I crumpled up the picture and threw it away in the garbage can outside my science class but held onto the note written in blood. I sat down at my desk and started to cry. My teacher came over to my desk to see if I was okay and saw the note.

He immediately became concerned and asked me what was going on. I told him my boyfriend had given it to me and it was written in his blood. We still had a few minutes before class started, so he escorted me to the principal's office. He told the principal it was urgent and showed him the note before returning to his class. The principal asked me for the story behind the note, and I told him that I had broken up with my boyfriend, and he gave it to me.

He called him into the office as well and asked for his side of the story. My boyfriend explained that he was in his robotics class and accidentally cut his finger, and so the blood dripped on the paper and smeared while he wrote in pencil but didn't think anything of it. There were light pencil markings under the blood to back up his story.

He then continued to tell the principal about the fake pregnancy, making the point that I was mentally unstable. In my defense, I brought up his leg and how he carved "I'm sorry, Skylynn" into it. The principal asked to see it, and so he rolled up his pant leg and showed us. "I'm not going to listen to a blaming match," the principal said. "You two sit in here while I contact your parents."

He sent the receptionist into the room to watch us. She sat between us on the other side of the table and stared, moving her gaze back and forth between us. There was an awkward tension in the air. The principal returned to the room and told us that our parents were on the way for a meeting with him and that we were expected to stay where we were until they arrived.

It was about a 20-minute wait in complete tense silence until they arrived. Then they deliberated, in front of us, about what they should do and how frustrating and dramatic teenagers are. Ultimately, they decided to separate us completely. This meant they had to rearrange our schedules so our paths would never cross during the day. They changed our lunch times and informed each teacher that we were to stay separated.

They got a school map and moved around our classes and times. When they were finished, both parents had to sign off on it. They also agreed to put us in counseling separately with the school counselor. Our new schedules were effective immediately. I had to give up my theater elective because he had it the next hour, and that put us too close. So, I enrolled in ROTC instead.

I wasn't allowed to walk home anymore. My parents clarified that they would pick me up every day, and I was to sit in the front office until they arrived. Before we left, the principal told my parents I was failing all my classes. I had hoped that he wouldn't have brought that up. I was ashamed of my grades and knew my parents would be disappointed. They were, and I was grounded until I got them up. I didn't care about bringing them up, so I stayed grounded for a while. Life wasn't about school anymore. Life wasn't about anything anymore.

The next few days were rough as I adjusted to a new schedule. I didn't get to keep any of my original classes or my lunch hour. He got to keep most of his classes and lunch. I didn't like talking to the school counselor either. She made me feel belittled and dramatic.

After the first session, I told her I pretended to be pregnant because he was hitting me. She didn't believe me and tried to dig into why I felt I needed attention. This became exhausting, and I stopped trying to heal altogether. I accepted that this was who I was now, and there was nothing I could do about it. He only went to two sessions in total and was released from counseling. He started telling everyone what I did to him and convinced our old friend group that I was manipulative and a whore. I became completely isolated and detached.

On the first day in my new science class, the lesson was about flowers and photosynthesis vs. cell division. The topic of sunflowers came up, and the teacher went on a lecture about them. He explained how young sunflowers rise from east to west, following the sun. Then at night, they reset, facing east, waiting for the sun to return. When they are fully grown, they only face east, not needing to chase the sun. This stayed with me. Was I a young sunflower, facing east in the dark, waiting for the sun to rise?

In ROTC, I was one of the only girls in the class, and I was the new girl. Most of the boys were seniors and had already heard that I liked attention and was a whore.

They'd wink at me and make provocative gestures. I ignored it the first couple of days, and then it escalated into sexual harassment. After a month in the class, I dropped out because of the harassment and took a different elective. I didn't tell anyone about the sexual harassment in ROTC because who would have believed me? And the boys knew that. I started to believe I was just a sex object for men and had no other purpose, just as my boyfriend had told me. I enrolled in photography for the rest of the year and kept completely to myself.

Out of the hope of being more understood, I showed my mother the poem I had written about suicide. She said, "That's very dark," and handed it back. I told her that's how I felt, and she told me I was being dramatic and I'd grow out of this attention-seeking phase. Since that didn't work, I turned my poem into my English teacher for a free writing assignment that was due the second day I started that class. She never gave it back, said anything, or reached out.

I felt completely alone and that the sun really would never rise. I stopped making plans for the future because I was certain that I would commit suicide by the time I was 18. My self-harm struggle intensified, and I started to feel like I missed him and that he was the only person who would ever love me.

I started to make friends with the wrong crowd and began to drink and do drugs. I got into sketchy situations with adult men and drug dealers, but I didn't care. I was so numb that I welcomed any adrenaline. I chased chaos.

Even though he and I were forced to be apart, he would still occasionally stand outside my bedroom window at night, wanting me to let him in. I wouldn't, so he started crawling through the dog doors to see me. Nothing changed when we were together, though. He would still hit and degrade me. I started locking the dog door at night, which stopped him from getting into the house. Occasionally I would see him ride his bike by my house, but that was the least of my worries.

For my sophomore year, the school was less strict about watching us. They still planned our schedules and alerted the teachers, but it was less intense. I was also permitted not to go to counseling anymore since she reported it wasn't helping me. I continued to have no friends and was still known as the attention whore. I started feeling like all the teachers and the counselor had given up on me.

Despite this, I got involved in an after-school club called Best Buddies. I did this to keep myself busy and away from my house. I became invested in it, and they asked me to do a presentation during a school assembly. I was nervous to talk in front of the whole school, that knew me as an attention-seeking person, but hesitantly, I agreed. As soon as I walked onto the floor during the assembly, in the silence, I could hear my ex yell out, "whore!" and the auditorium laughed. I shortened my speech and sat back down as fast as I could. That's how my fear of public speaking began. I quit the after-school club after that.

Outside of school that year, I convinced my parents to let me pick out a dog from the Arizona Humane Society. He was a Beagle and Jack Russell mix puppy brought into the shelter off of the street. I named him Eddie, and he became my best friend. He was a menace, though. He loved to kill birds, dig holes, eat clothes, and tear up furniture. Yet, despite all that, he loved to cuddle.

We would cuddle in my bed, on the couch, and even on the floor, and I would talk to him. I told him how my days went at school, what I was working on in classes, who was bullying me, and what emotions I felt.

He became my emotional support dog for many years because of his unconditional love. He knew when I was upset or crying, and he wouldn't leave my side. He comforted me in a way I hadn't felt in a long time.

He helped me cope with daily stress by being the reliable friend I always went home to, never leaving my side, always listening, and never judging me. When I had bad days, he would bring me my stuffed animals that he had ripped apart but knew I loved or bring me dead birds he had caught from outside. I needed him, and he was a critical part of my healing.

Junior year was easier because people had started to forget about me. I even got asked out by a boy, but I turned him down because I wasn't ready yet. I started making new friends and coming out of my shell. I tried to fit into friend groups but always felt out of place. I rejoined some of the clubs I had quit. I slowed down on drinking and drugs and slowly started to overcome my eating disorders independently. Yet overall, I was still struggling with thoughts of suicide.

I coped by immersing myself in art and music. I wrote more poetry and did more sketching and drawing.

All my writing and art were very dark in nature, but they helped me express my feelings. I also listened to songs on repeat that I related to and found comfort in them.

During senior year things got a lot better. I started to focus more on school and brought my grades up. I didn't worry about seeing him at all anymore. I made new friends, reconnected with old friends, and expanded my social circle. I even rejoined Best Buddies and a few other after-school clubs. I still didn't talk about my ex for fear of anyone remembering.

My class before lunch was as a student aid for a special education class. After class one day, I was walking with one of the girls to the lunchroom, and a "popular" girl tripped on her electric wheelchair. She immediately got infuriated and said a few offensive slurs, saying, "This is why you should have never been born." I was shocked. She was shocked and started crying uncontrollably. She didn't want to eat lunch in the cafeteria anymore, so I ate lunch with her in the classroom.

She was uncontrollable for most of the lunch hour but by the end told me how much she appreciated me and felt like no one ever really saw her or that she had a voice to be heard.

Her telling me that hit me hard, and I felt like I could relate. After that, my desire to be a strong advocate for people with disabilities increased, and I worked my way up to President of Best Buddies. I attended a leadership conference in Indiana to learn how to be a better advocate, friend, and listener. I never wanted anyone to feel the way I did, and I was going to stop it with all the fight I had in me.

In my English class, I discovered that the girl next to me was my ex-boyfriend's new girlfriend. Finding out that he had a new girlfriend sent me back into a deep depression. I tried to talk to her, be her friend, and then empathize and relate to her. We talked for a few days, but she shut me out as soon as I brought him up. I tried to empathize more and describe bruises no one else would know about, but she panicked and pushed me away further.

I became the "jealous ex," and no one believed me again. I shut it down faster this time and gave up right then and there. I couldn't go through it again, and I couldn't relive it through her.

It hurt me that I couldn't save her, but she didn't want to be saved, and I had to protect myself. I still talked to her from time to time, and we did group projects together. But we never talked about him again.

We made a friend group with another girl in that English class and became close friends. Sometimes I wonder if I tried to keep her close in case she needed to be saved or if I did it because I missed him. I think it was a mix of both.

I graduated senior year with A's again, although I still self-harmed and was suicidal. I did date a boy that year, but he was also toxic, and it didn't last long. I noticed that I started chasing red flags, almost like I was attracted to toxicity.

Outside of school that year, I started spending my time making jewelry. I liked it because it was a more tactile activity than writing and drawing. I grew from making jewelry to making backpacks and purses completely out of beads. I used it as a distraction from my life. My uncle, who lived with us, saw my projects grow, and he suggested I start my own business. He helped me get a tax and business license, and he helped me buy my beads wholesale. I named my company Kandi Korner.

We ended up being able to rent out a ten-foot by ten-foot space in a swap mart as well as a booth at an art walk called First Friday. I learned many business skills through this experience and am grateful that he took the time to help me with the process.

Creating and running Kandi Korner reminded me of the drive I used to have and inspired me to find it again. I realized I did want to be the girl I was before my abuser. I ended up breaking even every month with Kandi Korner, and with my mental, I could not continue my business longer than nine months.

After high school and moving out of my parent's house, I went to a free therapy program for women who experienced domestic violence. I did group classes on Wednesday nights and one-on-one sessions on Fridays. I learned coping skills to try to stop self-harming and how to cope with what happened to me. These classes were imperative to where I am today, and I'm glad I was brave enough to attend them. I later got diagnosed with PTSD and bipolar type 2 disorder stemming from PTSD.

Overall, I felt ashamed that I left that relationship, mentally- with new personality disorders and physically- with many scars. I had a torn tendon in my ankle, pencil graphite embedded in my skin, and a dislocated rib. The tear in my tendon is too small for surgery, so I have to try and provoke it to heal on its own, but I still have it to this day. The embedded graphite was eventually rejected and pulled out, but I had it in my skin for nine years.

The dislocated rib shows slightly, but there's no way of correcting it. I was on and off medications to help and stay mentally stable.

While talking with therapists, I realized the trauma was so intense that I had blocked out memories and could only remember specific instances. We worked together to open those locked doors, but even today, I have many partial memories of that time frame. They also treated me for depression, anxiety, insomnia due to night terrors, dissociation, and an eating disorder.

This process also brought to light unresolved childhood trauma. So, I learned coping skills to help heal my inner child and acknowledge what I went through. These classes also helped me learn how to talk to people without dumping negative feelings and trauma on them.

Although for me, that turned more into not talking much at all. I also continued to find healing in music and submersed myself in albums, specifically Badlands, released by music artist Halsey. I listened to this album on repeat for so long that it probably would've broken if it were a CD.

I got a tattoo of an ampersand over the scars on my wrist to remind myself that I had a story to tell and the rest of my story to write. It helped me remember the past, learn from it, and keep going. I also got a tattoo of a pocket watch with roses growing out of it on my back to symbolize how time heals, and with time roses bloom from buds into beautiful flowers. The clock points to 9:30 PM, which was the first time I stood up to him and yelled that Skylynn was dead because of him. The piece was going to include a blue sky and sunflowers mixed into the roses, but I never went back to have it finished.

Things started to get frustrating when I could recognize when I was self-sabotaging, but I didn't know how to stop it. I felt like someone else was controlling my actions, and I was just watching from the sidelines. I continued to find myself in toxic situations, even after I started dating a more stable guy than the guys I had previously dated.

I was enrolled in college but dropped out due to a relationship issue and didn't have the proper support to continue. I was struggling to figure out who I was, and he didn't have a clear vision of his future either. We weren't good for each other in the beginning.

We worked through it, partially because he was the best boyfriend I ever had and partially because I didn't know how to leave.

We stuck through the rough times and ended up getting married years later. I was still not the healthiest mentally, and because of that, I continued to struggle with putting myself in harm's way. Looking back now, I think I liked him saving me because I was never saved in my first relationship.

I struggled with getting rid of the things my ex had given me. I felt an attachment to them, and it physically hurt me to let them go. Through the years of dating, my husband helped me release all the items I still clung to. He helped me burn the notebooks and notes and throw away the rings. This helped me heal, grow, and find some confidence in myself again.

My marriage to him didn't last very long because, with his support, I came out as gay. In my journey of healing and self-awareness, I realized that my true self was attracted to females. Not because I had a grudge against men or my abuse, it had started before that; and that's the version of myself I was trying to find again. Who I was before—the confident, beautiful, carefree girl with big dreams.

I worked hard to control my destructive impulses and eventually did. I find myself still attracted to chaos and red flags, but I am better at controlling it and not giving in.

I lost a few critical relationships when I came out as gay, which slowed down my healing process and created doubt. I heard condescending statement after condescending statement. If I didn't have the support of my ex-husband and a few crucial friends, I would have gone back into the closet. I struggled with my choices internally for a long time and resorted to self-harm. I reached out to counselors and attended a few sessions to realign myself and regain control. Most of the relationships I lost originally, we have started to repair, but a couple of them are still immensely damaged.

Today, I am officially three years clean of self-harm. I have been in a healthy relationship for five years, and she and I are getting married in December. We met in my senior year of high school, and she was the third in my friend group in English class. We bonded over books because we both loved to read. We agreed that it was an escape from our realities. We remained friends over the years. After I came out as gay, I told her I had a crush on her since high school and asked her to be my girlfriend.

From the time we started dating to being engaged, we have created a beautiful life together. We go on adventures and explore together. We learn and grow together. We currently have six pets that we love and care for. We have my beagle Eddie who is now 14 years old, a dachshund Mickey that we adopted together, a cat we inherited from my relationship with my ex-husband named Kitty, two gerbils, and an axolotl. We take ballroom dancing classes together because we discovered a mutual love for dance and have no plans of stopping.

I am back in college and working towards a degree in accounting, and she is looking to take more classes to further her education. My goal is to be a successful businesswoman. I want to become someone my younger self would have been proud of and my teenage self would have never believed possible. After we are married in December, and after I am secure in my healing journey, we want to foster children because we both agree that we want to help the children that need families.

My fiancée has also helped me learn and grow over the past five years. She constantly reassures me that I am strong and capable. Because of her help, I am better at holding myself in public in a way that doesn't attract abusers.

Meaning that I learned how to identify my "tells" and correct them. Along with this, I can now fully identify when I am trying to revictimize myself and reach out for help confidently.

Today, I am still afraid of my abuser in some aspects because he did promise me he would always come back for me. I know I'm protected and safe now, but sometimes at night, if I see a shadow outside, my brain will briefly think it's him. Then I must breathe, let go of the anxiety, and continue with what I was doing. I've gotten much better at this over the years, but occasionally he still haunts me. Additionally, I no longer check his social media accounts or obsess over his current relationships. Most people who know me have no idea about what I went through. I am quiet, soft-spoken, professional, and optimistic; therefore, I carry myself well.

I struggled with my faith in religion throughout my journey. Even though I was raised in Christianity, I had to find my own relationship with God. I loved God throughout the relationship with my abusive ex-boyfriend until I asked Them for help. I asked for Them to see me or for *anyone* to see me and to make the abuse stop. Unfortunately, I received nothing, and at that point, I lost most of my faith. With the faith I had left, I was mad at God.

I was angry with Them for many years.

After I came out as gay, I lost the rest of my faith due to rejection from the Christian community. It was hard for me to believe in a hateful God because growing up, all I heard about was God's endless and unconditional love. Eventually, I found a community of open and affirming Christians that welcomed me with open arms. Because of them, I found security in rebuilding my relationship with God and now have a stronger relationship with Them than I did before.

Even though I have come so far in my healing journey over the years, I still have miles to go. But even so, I am not ashamed and am done hiding. I have surrounded myself with so much love and support. I have surrounded myself with people who listen to me and understand why I struggle so hard.

Even so, they will pick me up every time I fall. When I have bad days, weeks, or months, I remind myself to stand up tall and face the east just like a fully grown sunflower with no need to chase darkness. I don't worry about when the sun will rise again because I know it will. I am a survivor, and I am strong.

Kara Oakes
Email: thekaraoakes@gmail.com

About the Author

Kara Oakes lives in Eastern Oregon with her husband and their three thriving children. She graduated with a degree in Social Work which gave her the ambition to be involved in her community. She currently works as an Advocate at Project DOVE, her local domestic violence shelter. Kara is an avid minimalist. She enjoys party planning, volunteering at her kids' school, and going thrifting with her husband, Chad.

I am not a Frog

Urban legend says that if you put a frog into a pot of boiling water, the frog will jump right back out.

The frog knows it is wrong, it hurts, and it will kill him. But if you put the frog in a pot and slowly raise the water to boiling, he will stay. That is what abuse is like. You might not even notice that it is happening at first. I didn't. I brushed it off in so many ways until I was hot, and my skin was peeling, and I did not know if I even remembered that I could jump out of the pot.

An abusive person is not abusive all the time. They will demonstrate positive character traits most of the time. You have a lot of amazing days with them and only a few bad moments.

For me, that is what made the abuse so confusing when it did happen and what made leaving that much more difficult.

I did not start out that way. I was not a confused person. I came from a solid family with strong core values. My parents worked hard in life and loved each other very much. They passed that love on to my siblings and me.

I was very lucky to have an easy, happy childhood that was violence-free. I did not know what domestic violence even was. Maybe because of that, I was also naïve. I was just twenty years old when I met Benny. Old enough that I should have known better but too young to care.

I had just finished up my freshmen year of college at Dixie State University in St. George, Utah. I was there on an alumni scholarship and honestly had the perfect freshman college experience. I was ready for more, but my first stop to more was going back home to Idaho for the summer. There was a cute boy that I knew would also be at home for the summer.

We had been talking to each other on social media and through text. At twenty years old, I had only ever had one serious relationship.

The idea of going home for the summer and possibly having a summer boyfriend was very exciting for me.

It just so happened that my big sister and her husband knew Benny. They seemed happy that we had been talking and told me all about how great he was. That was all the confirmation I needed to start hanging out with him in person.

The day after I got into town, we decided to meet at the track in town at 5:30 in the morning so that we could go for a run together before it got too hot. I was immediately drawn to how humble of a person Benny was. We quickly fell into a routine that would last the whole summer. We would run together in the mornings, I would go to work, and whenever I was off, we would watch movies or go on drives. Benny made me laugh, and we shared a similar sense of humor. We never ran out of things to talk about. He was so nice and very sincere as a person.

Summer was ending fast, and it was almost time for me to return to St. George. That night we had gotten some ice cream. We were in a parking lot of a church building sitting in the back of his truck, enjoying our cold treat at the end of the hot summer day.

It was time for us to talk about what was going to happen when I left town in a couple of days. We both said how great of a summer it had been together and agreed that we did not want to say goodbye. We decided that we would be a long-distance couple. I would see him when I visited home on my breaks, and if he had time, he could come to visit me.

I had to get back to St. George ahead of the other students because that fall, I was going to be a Resident Assistant in the dorms. The first few days I was there, I had a lot of downtime until it was time for the residents of the dorms to show up. I was able to talk to Benny so much that it did not feel like we were living in two separate states. Once "back to school" week started, I got very busy.

The RAs went on an overnight retreat for team-building exercises and to get to know our team. When we got back, we did check-ins at the dorms. For three days in a row, I was up early, giving tours of the campus, showing students to their dorm rooms, and answering a thousand questions from worried and inquiring parents.

At the end of that week, I noticed a shift in Benny's overall attitude. I missed so many calls and text messages asking me what I was doing and why I had not answered the phone when he called.

I let him know I was just busy with my responsibilities as a resident assistant and that this was going to be how it was.

Benny said all the right things. He said he was worried about me when I took a long time to respond and that he just wanted to know that I was okay. It made me feel happy that someone cared that much about me. I did not want him to worry, so I respected his wishes. I checked in with him as often as I could after that, rather than waiting for the end of the day.

As I settled into my class schedule and work responsibilities, I became very good friends with Lacy and Justin. They were resident assistants just like me, and when we had to do our rounds of the dorms in the evenings, I was often paired with one of them. Because we had to do rounds at night, we were often up late, so we would go to Denny's and study between our rounds. I was doing exactly what I should have been doing as a college student. I was embracing the experience, making friends, and getting good grades.

Benny did not like it when I told him I was hanging out with Lacy and Justin instead of sitting in my dorm room talking to him on the phone. One night he lost it. He said he had been waiting for over two hours for me to call him.

He knew that I was out of class and had the time. He said that I was hurting his feelings and that Lacy and Justin were changing me, and he did not want that to happen to me. He said he missed me so much and that he just wanted to know that I missed him too. I liked Benny. I liked talking to him, and I knew that I did not like to make him upset. I thought it was nice that he was concerned about me.

Eventually, I started telling him that I was going to bed because I got up early. It was the perfect white lie. That way, I could still see Lacy and Justin, and I could still do my rounds without him having to know I was not asleep in my bed. I felt like it was emotionally draining to have open communication with Benny.

Around this time, I also befriended another resident assistant. His name was Julio. It was honestly a strange friendship. We met because we had the same job and had scheduled rounds at night together. Then I found out Julio was amazing at math, and math had always been my weakest subject. We began to meet in the Holland Building, and he would help me with my homework.

I liked Julio because he was nice. But I also needed to be his friend because I needed to pass my math class.

In an effort to be open and honest with my boyfriend back home, I told Benny that I was going to be studying with Julio when I needed help.

Benny told me that he did not want me to spend any time with Julio. He said that I didn't need Julio to help me because we could just do my math homework when I facetimed with him, and I would still get it done. I said okay, but in the back of my mind, I knew that this would be another thing that I hid from Benny.

I was in a situation that I did not understand. I was trying my best to do everything exactly as Benny wished but also omitting any part of my day that was not what he instructed me to do. It was not like me to feel like I needed to keep secrets. I thought I was being a good girlfriend by respecting his wishes and dedicating all my free time to Benny. That is what people did when they were in committed relationships, right?

Benny said that he loved me, and I liked the feeling of being loved. It was the first time anyone had ever told me that. He said he loved me, but I was walking on eggshells, unsure if I could tell him something without a blown-up, overly dramatic reaction.

I was going out of my way to make him happy, which was not easy because it was a long-distance relationship. I was not too worried about any of this though. I had been perfectly happy that summer, and I thought that it only seemed like he had changed because we were not together. I figured if I were still back home, everything would be fine.

Little did I know, a toxic cycle of abuse was just getting started. If I had known these controlling things Benny was doing were huge red flags, I might have questioned it. But I did not know any better.

Lacy and Justin asked me multiple times about my boyfriend back home. I told them all the good things. I did not feel that there was anything inherently wrong and did not bring up anything that would suggest there was. The term "abuse" was still not in my life's dictionary. I was not the frog in the boiling water yet, but I was the frog that had been caught, and unbeknownst to me, my turn in the pot was next.

November rolled around, and it was time for Thanksgiving break. To get home, I had to fly from Las Vegas, Nevada, to Boise, Idaho. Julio lived in Las Vegas and was going home.

I felt that we were good enough friends that I could ask him for a ride from St. George to the airport in Vegas.

It was about a two-hour car ride. When we got to the airport, I gave Julio my share of the gas money. He helped me unload my bag from his car, and I was on my way home. I had lied to Benny. For all he knew, I had had a very boring ride to the airport from a taxi service. I know I could never tell him that Julio had been the one to take me. This was the first time I felt physically afraid to tell Benny something. I knew it had to be my secret.

When I walked out of my terminal at the Boise airport and saw Benny there waiting for me, I was beyond happy to see him. I had missed him so much! The precious few days I had home for Thanksgiving were just what I needed. I spent some time with my family and some time with Benny's family. The whole time felt just like the summer. Benny and I were happy, we did not fight, and he didn't have to ask me where I was or what I was doing because he was right there with me the whole time. The relationship felt easy and reaffirmed my thoughts that things would be so different if we were not separated from each other. For those five days, I was happy.

From Thanksgiving until the end of the year was a little rough. I did not feel like a long-distance relationship was working for me. I did not think Benny was the problem. I thought that the distance was the problem and that if we were only in the same place, he wouldn't be so worried about me and therefore, would not be so controlling and demanding. I decided that I would not stay in St. George any longer. Being with Benny was more important to me.

I gave the housing manager at Dixie my notice that I would not be coming back to be an assistant after the break. I took my finals in mid-December, and then I packed up my dorm room and went home. In just four short months, I went from a dedicated college student to a college dropout. I wanted to keep Benny's Love more than I wanted to be a college graduate.

You can imagine my mom and dad's surprise and mild disappointment when I told them I was home for good. However, at the time, my mom's health was declining. She had been battling cancer for the past seven years and was not doing well. So, I was able to fly under the radar as my mom's health took my family's attention, and nobody asked me what my plans were. I do not think anyone knew I was as serious about Benny as I was.

They probably assumed I was afraid to leave my mom. They never guessed that I had changed my whole life plan for a boyfriend.

I will admit I missed the weather in St. George. I missed Lacy and Justin, and I missed my classes. Benny was there for me, though. He helped me pick up the pieces and made me feel like I was his number one priority. In mid-January, my sweet mother passed away from her cancer. Benny was there for that too. He never left me alone and was my shoulder to cry on. He took some time off work to stay with me during the day and made sure that I would be okay.

He listened any time I needed to talk about my mom, whether it be her life, things I loved about her, the things I was going to miss, and how sad I was that she had died. He loved me through one of the hardest times of my life. I could not have asked for anything more.

In April, I found out that I was pregnant. I was excited to have a baby. But I was not sure how Benny was going to take the news. When I told him, he said that we should not tell anyone yet, that it would be better if it was our secret. I decided that it was early enough and that there was no harm in that. In fact, it was probably better if I did not say anything anyways until I was closer to twelve weeks along.

I expressed to Benny my desire to be a family and that even though we had not really planned on having a baby, it was okay, and we could do it together. Benny came back with this wild idea that we should elope, and again it could be our secret. I did not understand why he wanted it to be that way, but after everything he did for me, I was more than happy to do something for him. I decided we could do this whatever way he wanted to. We got married on a random Thursday evening. When I told my dad about it, he asked me if I was happy. I told him I was because I had no reason to believe I wasn't.

We did not take a honeymoon. We just went right to real life. Benny and I would go to work every day, and when I got home, I would make dinner. Benny was an avid dirt bike rider. It was late spring, almost summertime, and he would often go ride his bike after dinner. He had a separate group of friends from me, which was fine, but it got to the point where he would skip dinner with me and go straight with his friends right after work. I hardly saw him.

One day I came home from work, and I was so tired from being pregnant. I figured Benny was not going to be coming home, so I decided not to cook dinner and just go to bed. Well, I was wrong, and Benny did come home.

He roughly woke me up from my nap to ask me when dinner was going to be ready. I told him I was not cooking, and without saying a word, Benny just left. He left and did not come home until the next day after work. When he returned, he gave me the silent treatment for the whole week. This behavior was strange to me and did not sit right, but I also was not sure how much of a problem it was. There are always worse things than that, right?

Two months later, in July, not only was the honeymoon phase over for me, but I was beginning to pick up on a pattern of power and control. I knew that I did not like it, but I still did not have a name for it. I wanted some space to try and clear my head. I texted my older sister and asked if I could go to her house. She asked me if I regretted getting married, and I said yes. She let me spend the night.

The first night, Benny did not even ask me where I was. He did the second night, and he said if I just came home, we could work it out-- that he would come home after work and spend time with me. He apologized for his behavior, and I accepted the apology.

After I got back, Benny came up with this master plan. I would give back the vehicle my dad was letting me borrow, quit my job and stay home and get ready for the baby to come.

He said he was busy at work, that we would for sure be able to make it on one income, and he wanted me to stay with our baby girl. I was excited about that. I was more than happy to take on the role of being a homemaker. I thought it was a great plan. I put in my two weeks at my job, and after the two weeks, I gave my dad back his vehicle.

The same evening, I was at home in bed. Benny came home from wherever he had been that night and had a gift for me that his aunt had given us for the baby. Rather than waking me up and handing me the gift, he threw it at me.

I was sound asleep, and the next thing I knew, a gift bag filled with baby items hit me in the face. I was officially a frog that had been put in a pot of water. I thought I would be taking care of my home and family. In reality, I was now in a position where I depended completely upon a person that did not see me as an equal life partner.

I had a desire to be a good wife, regardless of what our problems were. I did everything for him and was willing to do anything. I believe that Benny knew this and took advantage of me. At first, it came across as him being emotionally needy. Every day was just another day in an endless cycle of catering to whatever Benny needed. Honestly, this was like trying to fill up a bottomless pit.

Slowly he became entitled. No matter what I did for him, it was never enough. He would come up with more demands for me to meet because he believed that his needs were my responsibility. He quickly drained me down to nothing. The first time I experienced verbal abuse was on a Sunday. We were getting ready to go to my parent's house for Sunday dinner. That morning, we had an argument that ended with him calling me a very specific, degrading name that I knew did not deserve to be called.

I thought to myself: "did he really just call me that?" I told myself that he did not mean it; he was just mad. Benny left the house, and I went to Sunday dinner alone. It was common for me to always be at family events by myself. At first, everyone would ask me where Benny was. I always felt the need to defend him. Eventually, my family members must have accepted that he would never come with me because they stopped asking. I was grateful I did not have to keep lying for him.

Once the verbal abuse was occurring regularly, it opened the door for a lot of other things. Not only was I a frog in the water, but the heat had just been turned up. When it was time for me to have my first baby, I let Benny know.

I had not been feeling well and had gone to bed; it was bedtime anyway. I realized that I was having contractions, but they were not anywhere close to 5 minutes apart, so I decided I was going to wait it out and just go to sleep.

Around ten, I got up and went out to the living room to tell Benny that I was having contractions and that I was pretty sure it was the real thing. He didn't even take his eyes off the television and just said okay. I went back to bed. Around midnight Benny finally came in to go to sleep.

I was awake and told him I was still having contractions and that they were becoming more frequent. I said it might be time to go to the hospital, but I was unsure. Rather than helping me figure it out, Benny said he was going to sleep because he was tired and to wake him up if something more happened. By 3:00 am that morning, my contractions were 10 minutes apart, and I began throwing up. Benny waited until I was puking and could barely walk to finally agree that I should go to the hospital.

He took me to the hospital, where I was already dilated to a five and in active labor. He stuck with me through it. I had a very fast labor. Our first baby was born at 8:00 a.m.

Benny never even held the baby. Once the labor was over and the baby was out, he said he was going home to shower and get some breakfast and would be back. He did not come back though.

Throughout the day, I texted him asking him when he would be back. I told him that the nurses needed to complete the paperwork, we needed to name the baby, and I was waiting for him. He never responded and disappeared for the entire day. On what should have been a very happy day, the exciting birth of a baby, being a mom for the first time, and having a beautiful daughter, I was feeling so devastated.

I gave everything I had to Benny every single day. The one day that I needed him to come through for me, he did not. I was not a priority to him. So many times, I experienced my abuser withholding the emotional connection that I needed. Domestic violence is painful. It is absolutely soul-crushing to be abused by a person you love and think loves you back.

Time went on. I was at home with my baby, and there was no other place I wanted to be. As far as my marriage went, I chalked it up to a rough patch.

I figured that every couple goes through things, and whatever this was, it was our thing to go through. I put all my energy into being the best mom I could be and did my best to maintain Benny's expectations of me.

I did everything I could to not do or say anything that would make him upset with me. If there was no conflict, we were okay. In fact, we got along so well with no conflict that I found myself pregnant with baby number two when my first baby was six months old.

When I told Benny, he was happy. He said two kids would be so fun and so perfect. I thought we might reach a turning point soon and figure out our differences, or whatever it was that sometimes made things so difficult.

A few months later, my child spilled some apple juice on the kitchen floor. My husband called for me to come into the room, and then he put his hands on me and physically pushed me down to the floor so that I could mop it up. I was nine months pregnant at the time. I thought to myself, "did he really just do that?" I told myself that he did not mean it and that I needed to be a better housekeeper. He said he was sorry and he would not do that to me again.

A week later, it was nighttime, I was asleep, and I woke up because Benny was aggressively rubbing his wet socks on my face. When I opened my eyes, he started yelling at me and said he had stepped in water and now his socks were wet. He made me get out of bed and clean up the water. I cried, and he apologized after a while. He said he was not going to act that way anymore.

We found out we were having a boy. Benny was so excited to have a son. The day I went into labor, I knew before Benny even left for work that today was going to be the day. I told him what signs I was having that I knew labor had started and told him it was going exactly the way my first labor had gone, and I knew it would be soon. He said he was going to go to work anyways.

You can imagine my disappointment in thinking it would be a good day, only to feel the same rejection I felt when I had my first baby. I said I needed to take our daughter to an appointment in a couple of hours, and I needed the car that day. He let me take him to work, knowing I was in labor. I am a religious person, so I prayed hard that I could do what I needed to do that day before the baby came out.

I was so isolated by that time that reaching out to someone for help did not even feel like an option. I had so many family members and people at my church that would have helped in a heartbeat if they had known I was in labor and my daughter had a doctor's appointment. Looking back, it breaks my heart that Benny had that much control over my everyday life.

I took Benny to work and then got my daughter to the doctor. During that time, I had an occasional contraction, maybe two or three an hour. At my daughter's appointment, the doctor said that she would need a prescription. I thought to myself, okay, well, I probably have time for that; the contractions are not bad yet. I went to Rite Aid, but the prescription was not ready. I had about a 30-minute wait.

During the wait, I realized my contractions were getting stronger. I don't know how I kept my one-year-old entertained for what ended up being 45 minutes in Rite Aid while in active labor, but I did it. As soon as I had that prescription in hand, I drove straight to my husband's job and told him we needed to go. That was around 2:00 p.m. We dropped our daughter off at my sister's house.

On our way to the hospital, Benny said that he had not had time to eat lunch, and it was past lunchtime.

He said he was going to stop at McDonald's and asked if I wanted anything. I sat there in the front seat of the car, with contractions coming 7 minutes apart, while my husband ate his food.

It was 4:30 by the time we checked into the hospital, and my son was born just after 6:00 p.m. Once again, after the birth was over, Benny was nowhere to be seen. He said he had scheduled a ride along with the fire department that night and had stuff to do. Once again, I was my most vulnerable and really needed him, and his actions showed me exactly how much I meant to him.

My son was born in April, and from April to October was one of the worst time periods of abuse during my four-year marriage to Benny. I remember a sunny Saturday afternoon, my daughter, who was 18 months old, was taking her afternoon nap. I was sitting on the couch, breastfeeding my new three-month-old baby. Benny was walking around pointing out the messes in the house from the kids and asked when I planned on picking things up. I told him I would get to it when the baby was done nursing.

Benny then started picking up the objects laying around the house and began to throw them directly at me. A sippy cup, a wooden spoon from the kitchen drawer, a couple of baby toys, and a shoe.

Then he stormed out the door without any other conversation. After he left the house, I sat there thinking, "did that really just happen?" "What if he had hit the baby?" Once again, I downplayed the situation and told myself he did not mean it.

Suddenly all the bad name calling, the intimidation, and the heavy criticism did not seem so bad anymore because now he was hitting me. By telling myself that he did not mean it and brushing it off each time, I minimized what was really taking place. I reduced all those moments to the smallest degree that I could. I said things like:

"The situation wasn't that bad."

"If only I would have...."

"Maybe I'm just overreacting."

"He's doing his best."

"It could have been worse."

"Maybe this is what I deserve."

"It will get better if I stay silent."

These statements are examples of gaslighting. I was so used to Benny gaslighting me that I was gaslighting myself! These phrases I repeated to myself more times than I can count to justify Benny's actions toward me. His behavior got worse and more frequent over time, and gaslighting myself was my main coping mechanism to get through it.

In the middle of all of this, we got new neighbors on the other side of the duplex that we lived in—a young couple just like us. The girl's name was Heather. She was at home all day with her kids, just like I was. We became fast friends. If there is one thing about me, it's that I don't easily make friends; I never have. Heather was a blessing to me. She would randomly pop over in the mornings and say hi. We would sit and talk while I folded laundry, and she would do my dishes or hold my baby. Sometimes I would go next door, and we would watch movies while the babies napped.

When summer hit, she and her husband put up a nice big pool on their side, and we swam every day that summer. It was the adult friendship I dreamed of having and the one bright spot in my life. Heather saw things, though. She saw the way that I changed when Benny was around.

She said it was not right to always be walking on eggshells and to have to work so hard for his love. She saw how isolated I was. She heard our fights through the duplex walls, and she heard when he threw things.

Heather helped me put a definition to what was happening. It was abuse. She told me not to let him treat me that way. I agreed that I did not want to live the way I was living, but I also knew that any time I put my foot down and tried to stand up for myself were the times that Benny got his angriest. There was not a simple answer to my problem, but at least I had a definition for it.

One night I was having a super tough time getting my one-year-old to bed. It was late, way past bedtime, and as usual, Benny was not anywhere to be found. I was desperate, so I asked Heather if she could take the baby for me while I got my one-year-old to bed. Heather came right over and took the baby back to her side of the duplex.

I had just barely finished getting my precious little girl to sleep and was about to get the baby when Benny finally got home. It was nearly midnight. The first thing he asked was where the kids were. I began to explain what happened and why Heather had the baby.

Benny said that he did not trust Heather. Heather was crazy, and she was not a good influence on me. I was confused as to why Benny would say these things, and I told him all the things Heather did for me and how great of a friend she had been. Benny told me to go next door and get the baby now and that I was never allowed to let her watch our kids again.

After that, Benny started coming home at random times. He would come on his lunch break when he never did before to try and catch me with Heather around. He would come home from work right on time or even early just to see what we were up to. It got awkward. If I were next door, he would come knock on the door and say he needed me to come home. If Heather was over, he would awkwardly make everyone uncomfortable with his presence so that she would go home.

It got to the point where we would talk to each other if we were both outside on the shared front lawn, but other than that, neither one of us dared to do anything else. Heather did not want him to get angry with me because of her, and I did not want to cause any sort of contention to have to deal with. Benny could not just let it stop there, though.

About a month later, he came home and informed me that our landlords had a second duplex, and a tenant of theirs was moving out. He said we would be moving to a different duplex starting the next day. I was devastated. I needed Heather, and just as fast as I had her, Benny took her away from me. He wanted me to know that he was in charge.

Heather changed my life. I had a lot of family members around, but I had already been isolated from them for so long that nobody came over. I saw them at Sunday dinners and major family events. During these times, either I was alone, or Benny had turned on his charm again. The charm that everyone knew. My family did not know what was going on, but Heather saw it. Heather had a front-row seat.

Once she helped me put a name to my problems, I started thinking about it a lot more. Domestic violence can be defined as a pattern of behavior used by one partner to gain or hold power or control over the other. The abuse can be physical, emotional, psychological, or economic, and includes any behavior that manipulates, intimidates, humiliates, isolates terrorizes, coerces, or hurts someone (Un.org).

I learned what abuse was and could finally match up incidents with the definition. I was able to finally see what the definitions looked like in real life.

It looked like:

- Breaking my laptop and blaming the kids.
- Having to first ask him for money and then give him both the receipt and the change after I went to the store.
- The time he threw away my whole makeup bag with everything in it simply because he wanted to hurt my feelings.
- He told me lies about my friends at church so that I would not want to go, and if I did, I would not want to talk to anyone.
- Not giving me any gas money and keeping me at home. Telling me lies about my family and isolating me from them.
- Asking me where I was all the time.
- Not giving me access to his bank accounts.
- Not adding me to his health insurance plan.
- A lot of mind games.
- He used to move things around, so I could not find what I needed.
- He would pretend he did not know where the item was, watch me look everywhere for it, and then tell me I was losing my mind.

Eventually, I really did think I was going crazy.

Benny's mood changes were especially confusing. He could be a different person from day to day or even from hour to hour. At times he was aggressive and intimidating, his tone was harsh, and his words were insulting. When he was in that mode, nothing I said or did would seem to have any impact on him except to make him angrier. My side of the argument would count for nothing, and everything was my fault.

He twisted my words around, and I always ended up feeling defensive and feeling like I could not do anything right. He constantly called me names. He would get into sudden rages with lots of swearing and yelling. He lied to me all the time and could not go through a single conversation without blaming me or belittling me. I came to expect being given the silent treatment and him withholding affection from me.

Add in the threats and isolation and nonstop gaslighting, and I was barely functioning. I was mentally and emotionally broken, unable to recognize my value as a person, unsure of myself, and unable to trust anyone or anything. I was in survival mode, and I became very good at predicting his moods and what his actions were going to be.

I believed that if I was agreeable and did everything exactly the way he wanted, I would be safe, but that was not true.

All marriages are sacred, but not all are safe. I was sure that I was not safe in my marriage. After what happened when I talked to Heather, I felt that I could not talk to anyone without even more being taken from me, even though I barely had anything anyways. When he finally graduated from throwing things at me to physically hitting me, I tried to find some courage. I told him that if it happened again, I would leave. I knew that it was wrong, but I did not know how to stop it other than to threaten him back.

Benny promised me over and over that it would not happen again, and I believed him. It only got worse. He would react badly at the tiniest things, like when his dinner was cold or his work uniform was wrinkled.

One time I got a phone call from a friend I still had in St. George. It was random and the first time I had heard from them in almost two years. When I got off the phone, Benny pinned me against the wall and told me if I ever talked to them again, he would shoot them. I told him I was sorry and that I would listen to him. He told me he was protecting our relationship and I needed to trust only him.

My home did not feel like it belonged to me. He made me feel like I was lucky to be allowed in his home. I could not do anything that he would consider out of line because I lived in fear of him. My life did not feel as important as his. I felt like I was not worthy or good enough for anything; it did not matter what it was.

I felt like I did not deserve anything, and everything I did was wrong. Everything I said was criticized. It was like he remembered everything I said and saved my words to use against me later. I felt humiliated every single day. I lived in misery, but my suffering was never valid. I was used and then discarded. My needs were never on the table.

By this time, I was fending for myself, even though I had a husband. The longer he withheld my needs from me, it forced me to find a way to get the items that I needed. I sold my personal belongings on social media. When I had nothing left to sell, I began babysitting for Benny's cousin Jennifer to earn money.

Luckily for me, Benny did not mind it. I made just enough to be able to get diapers and wipes every month and whatever else my babies needed. What was leftover I would spend on myself.

There was never enough for everything that I needed at one time. I often had to choose between two basic choices. Did I want to have new deodorant, or did I want to shave my legs? Did I want new shoes for the winter, or would I rather have a sweater?

One miserable winter, I had been to my dad's house for Sunday dinner, and he noticed I wasn't wearing a coat. A few days later, he stopped by and said he had an early Christmas present for me. He had bought me a nice new coat. I was so grateful to him and also so embarrassed at the same time that my life was such a mess that I didn't even have a coat to wear. I never ever said out loud that my husband was not providing for me. I let my dad make his own conclusions, and I kept doing my duty as a wife and defending Benny.

As time went on, Jennifer picked up on some things. She casually started asking me a few questions here and there and bringing up her own experiences with past relationships when she would come to pick up her child after work. After a while, I realized that I could trust her and opened up to her just enough to say that I needed help.

She had a friend who worked at Project DOVE and told me that was where I needed to go. I made an appointment, did my intake with Cecelia, and went home.

I thought about all the things that we talked about during the intake and ended up calling her back later that afternoon. I told her I wanted to stay in the shelter.

She said that she had gotten special permission to come and get me because I was unable to transport myself there. I remember feeling so humbled that I was important enough to her that she was willing to put herself in that situation to come back and get me. We moved quickly. She loaded up the kids while I grabbed as many diapers and wipes as I could.

While we were getting in the car, Cecelia asked if I would have any neighbors that would tell Benny that they saw me loading up a couple of things and leaving. I told her no because I had not dared to make any new friends on this street. As far as I knew, no one even knew I was there. That was the reality of the life I was living.

I went to the shelter, but shelter life is hard and takes commitment. I was not ready. On one hand, if I had to be locked up somewhere, at least I was safe. However, I was still in the habit of minimizing my abuse. It was hard for the advocates to help me because I was not ready to admit that I was in an abusive relationship, much less do anything about it.

Packing up and leaving was fine, but I had been gaslighting myself for so long that I was not able to visualize what life was beyond right now. I could not see what life would look like away from my abuser. I lacked the ability to make any decisions because for so long, I was not able to make any choices. Benny had not allowed me my most basic rights for so long that I did not know what to do when I was not being controlled.

At that time, I also found out that I was pregnant again with my third child. After two weeks of living in the shelter without much progress, I went back home. Benny promised me if I came back, things would be different. He said he was drinking too much, and that was making him mad at me. He said that he would stop. He said he was excited about a third baby and missed us the two weeks we were gone. I accepted his apologies. I believed in the promises he made to me.

We celebrated our fourth anniversary shortly after that, in May. Usually, the day was just like any other day, but that year he bought me some flowers. It was a big surprise. I wanted to feel loved, but I was so shocked that he would do something nice for me.

He never bought me anything, let alone something as "frivolous" as flowers. I could not even enjoy it because it was so out of character for him that I questioned it.

How long was he going to be nice for? Is this kindness being given to me with strings attached? Will I regret accepting them later? Are we finally going to have a turning point where things get better? Maybe he was not lying this time.

I got my answer to that when I was folding laundry. He was mad at me for something. I tried to walk away and not engage in the fight he was picking. He blocked the doorway and would not allow me to leave the room. He forced me to sit there while I listened to all his critical comments and names that he had for me. Later I threw those beautiful flowers in the trash. They never meant anything.

Summer came and went that year, and it was time to have my third baby. That day my family was having a birthday party for my youngest brother at 5:00. It was a Saturday, and earlier that day, I thought I was starting labor. Still, I thought I had time to go to the party. Around 2:00 pm, I texted Benny and told him that today was the today. I did not get a response, but I knew that he would have seen the message.

I went to the party knowing I had had a few contractions, but I wasn't worried about it. The party started at 5:00, and by 6:30, I was having contractions 10 minutes apart. I did not feel like I could tell my family I needed help. I was physically in the room with people who loved me and would have done anything for me. Yet I was so emotionally isolated that I could not even tell my own dad, or my brothers and sisters, that I was in labor.

I wanted Benny to be there for me, and I also knew that he would not want me to tell anyone else. I told my family I was feeling a bit nauseous and was going to go home. On my drive to my house, I realized my contractions were already 5 minutes apart. I called my sister and asked her to come to my house to watch my kids, but I did not tell her about my contractions. She said she would be right behind me.

I called Benny and said it was time. He said to meet him at home, and once my sister got there, he would take me to the hospital. I got home, and my sister had also arrived. Benny still had not shown up. I desperately wanted to believe he would show up for me this time. The third time is the charm, right?

I waited for him until I felt an overwhelming need to push. I knew the time to go to the hospital had come and gone. I called the one person I could think of who lived just down the street from me and went to my church, Sondra. I was so relieved that she had answered the phone that I started crying. I told her I needed a ride to the hospital.

It was a surreal feeling to be asking for the help I needed while still not feeling like I could even ask for help. As we walked to her car, she asked me about my contractions. I told her they were five minutes apart. We began walking to her car, and just from my front door to her vehicle, I had three contractions.

She looked at me and said, that is way closer than 5 minutes apart. I said I knew, but I didn't want her to worry. She got me to the hospital, and I asked if she could stay with me. I told her I didn't want to be alone. The baby was born 22 minutes later.

Benny showed up after everything was over. Sondra excused herself and left. Benny stayed with me for a little while, but not without demanding an explanation of why Sondra had been there. There I was, having just delivered a baby and in a particularly vulnerable place emotionally.

Benny told me that I had ruined the date that he was on. He had been out with another girl and was sorry, but he had to finish that up before coming to the hospital. Needless to say, he left. I was told I would have to stay in the hospital an extra day to monitor the baby. Benny left me alone in the hospital for the entire two days. We picked the name for our baby over text messages. He showed up right at my discharge time to take me home and drop me off.

My breaking point came about four months later. Things were getting bad at home. Benny had quit his job in October without much of a plan. We were at home together all day, and it was hard. I was walking on eggshells and never got a break from it like I would when he went to work. I did not know if it was going to be a good day or a bad day. I had to wait for him to wake up and then judge what his mood was.

In December, one of my best friends from high school posted on social media that she had lost her baby and would be having a funeral service. I decided that I wanted to attend the funeral, and I asked Benny if he would watch the kids so I could go. At that time, our children were four months, one and two years old.

I had finished getting myself ready to go, which was impressive given the fact that I had three kids under two. I decided I would try and get the baby to sleep before I left. Benny came into the bedroom and said to me, "Look at all the stuff I just cleaned up in ten minutes!" I said, "I am literally about to leave. If I weren't headed out, I would have just picked all that up."

He did not say anything else but reached out and pushed me backward. I was still holding the baby. By the time I regained my balance, he was standing next to me again, holding onto my arms. Knowing he was going to push me again, I begged him to let me put the baby down. He looked right into my eyes and said that I just needed to control my balance and everything would be fine. He then pushed me two more times.

That was what it took for me to realize that he really did not care about what he was doing. Until that point, I had been unable to understand that Benny was choosing to be abusive. That day he had the opportunity to do the right thing, but he did not. He chose to push me. He chose *not* to let me put my baby down where she was safe. He chose *not* to care about who was going to get hurt. The irony of the situation that day killed me.

Here was my good friend Kate and her husband **Tobby**, who were amazing parents and lost their baby due to no fault of their own. Then there was me, with more babies than I needed at one time, and as much as I tried to be the best mom I could, they were in harm's way. For the first time, I was thankful to be going to a funeral because then I could just sit there and cry as much as I needed to, and nobody would even think anything of it because everyone else in the room was crying too.

After that morning, I knew I could not let anything like that happen again. It was not fair to me, it was not fair to my children, and it wasn't fair to people like Kate. Two days later, I was back at Project DOVE, asking for help. It was not easy. I was embarrassed to be doing a new intake and having to admit to the same advocate the things that had happened since the last time we talked.

I was humiliated over the idea of coming into the shelter for a second time. I did not even want to make eye contact with my advocate because I felt ashamed. Cecelia told me it would be hard, but the time to do something was now. Interestingly enough, Benny and I were two months behind on rent at the time, and our landlords had given us an eviction notice.

To some, it would be a coincidence. To me, it was the miracle I had been praying for. You see, I desperately wanted out, but there was no way that Benny was going to allow me to just walk away. I wouldn't be able to simply choose to leave; I would have to escape. I knew that, and he knew that. I was afraid of what he would do if I tried to leave again. With an eviction thrown in the mix, Benny had no choice but to let me take the kids and go. He did not have anywhere to keep me anymore.

As a short-term fix, I moved in with my dad and tried to adjust to not having my day-to-day life controlled. I had been so isolated from my family that it was an adjustment for me to be able to be around them so much. They felt like strangers to me at first, but I quickly realized how much they loved me and how much they cared about my kids. I could not help but feel like I had to earn my spot back in my family and that once I did, it would be okay to let them in again and let them help me and support me.

As I continued working with my advocate, I eventually moved into the shelter's transitional housing with my three children. In addition to my family, I now had the staff at Project DOVE to help me pick up the pieces of my life.

The whole experience humbled me, which is almost laughable. It is not like an abused woman needs to be humbled any more than she already has been. The best part is that I stayed this time. I stayed gone. I finally remembered I could jump out of the pot of water that was boiling me.

Overcoming something like abuse does not just happen overnight. It takes baby steps every single day. Positive baby steps. I may have been able to remove myself from my situation physically, but I was still heartbroken. I mourned the loss of the family unit I had hoped to have. I was scared to be a single mom. Nobody in my immediate circle of people I knew were single parents.

I felt like I was failing. I worried about everything. I had a lot of anxiety. I had no idea how I would come up with the strength to put my life back together. All I knew was that my children needed me to.

Domestic violence had a significant impact on my health and well-being for those first few years that I was on my own. As the abuse got worse, I began to experience tension headaches, blurry vision, and recurring back pain. Those things did not stop just because I left the relationship.

I had to push through all that in the hopes that it would all lessen the longer that I was away from my relationship and the stress that came with it.

I also had to deal with the psychological effects of what I went through. I dealt with some depression, poor social skills from being isolated, feeling ashamed that my partner was abusive, suffering from a significantly diminished self-perception, and binge eating. For me, binge eating developed as a way for me to manage my unmanageable life. Where others might turn to drugs or alcohol to numb themselves, I chose to eat.

And guess what? Just like with the abuse, I also minimized all these effects of trauma. I have had to work hard mentally not to gaslight myself, to accept what my reality was, and to deal with it. I had allowed myself to be dominated by Benny for so long that I had lost all respect for myself. I have had to work hard to get it back.

The physical violence had been eliminated, but it did not mean that my abuser was any less dangerous to me. Leaving also did not mean that I was any less trapped either. After a few months in transitional housing, Benny showed up at the door. I was surprised he knew where I was, and I was dumb enough to let him come in.

He played with the kids for a few minutes, and I remember standing there nervously with my back against the wall, unable to sit down because I was so uneasy having him in the same room as us. The kids started fighting over a toy, as kids do, and Benny's reaction was to hit my son. He slapped him across the face, and when I asked him why he did that, he told me that he would not allow his son to be mean to girls (his sisters). I told Benny he needed to leave, that my unit was on Project DOVE's cameras, and if the advocates saw his car there, they would call the police.

He left, and I cried. I was devastated over that incident, and I realized that it would take a lot more than just separating from Benny to overcome this. I would have to put in some hard work to set boundaries up that were never there before.

Shortly after that, I got my first apartment. It did not take long for Benny to figure out where I was. He did not come around for the kids and barely saw them. He would come around to keep playing games with me. One night he showed up after ten p.m. and wanted to see the kids. I said the kids were in bed; they were all asleep. He started accusing me of keeping the kids from him.

When I realized we were about to start fighting, just like when we were married, I told him he needed to leave. He kept going, and I repeated four or five times that he needed to leave. I thought I was going to have to call 911. He stopped talking and stared at me for a few seconds, then turned and walked out. On his way out the door, he grabbed my car keys.

I saw him grab the keys, and I followed him out the door. I started yelling for him to give them back. He threw them as far as he could across the grass at the apartment building. It was 11 o'clock at night and pitch-black outside. I waited until he left, and then, with tears pouring down my face, I went out into the grass with the flashlight on my phone, looking for my keys. I wondered if this is what leaving looked like. Would he ever just stop? Do I really deal with this for the rest of my life?

Getting divorced was a tricky thing. I tried to make it his idea. I told him that we both knew our marriage was far less satisfying than either of us wanted or deserved. I told him that I appreciated him and the time we had while it was still good. I said I wanted a divorce and that it would be better for him to not to be tied to me anymore.

He said he would sign the divorce papers if, and only if, we did not use lawyers, did it ourselves, and basically did everything that he wanted. He would let me have the kids (how nice of him). They would continue living with me full time, so I did not care about anything else. I did the divorce his way. I was not ready to face him. I did not want to ask if he knew he had abused me. I didn't want any conflict. If we finally got divorced, I didn't care. I longed to be free of him.

My time as a single mom was not always easy and was incredibly lonely at times. Yet it was uplifting for me to be on my own in my apartment. I did not mind the responsibilities of paying rent and other bills because I had the ability to make sure those things got done. I had the power to choose where my money went, and with that, I had the peace of mind knowing that my kids and I would be taken care of. I could finally go to the store and get what I needed and not think twice about it.

Yes, as a single mom, money got tight, but I always made it work. My kids and I had stability and did not have to cater to Benny. We had some really great times, just the four of us. We did not have to walk on eggshells 24/7. The everyday tension had disappeared.

We all slept better. My little ones quit having nightmares. They found their voices. We learned that we could wake up happy and have a good day every day. I began to see that life is too short and beautiful to live trapped and abused, hiding under an umbrella of shame. We have so many happy memories from that apartment. To this day, whenever we drive past our old apartment building, the kids will start telling stories from our time there, and we all start laughing.

They say that on average, it takes a victim seven times to leave before staying away for good. This turned out to be true for me. The first time I went to my sister's house. That lasted two days. I went to my dad's house twice and the shelter once. There were also the times that I left mentally. Where in my head I was gone, but I just did not quite know how I would physically be able to make that happen.

I really do not like to use the word "survivor" in reference to myself. I know it is a popular blanket term, but to me, it feels like a very dramatic way to say that I have been through a situation. In some ways, I still downplay what happened. Because I have children with my abuser, there is a forever tie that will bind us together and leave the door open for continued conflict.

The required contact with Benny for the sake of our children does not make me feel like a survivor. Instead, I feel like I have been walking on a treadmill for four years, stuck in a continual loop of looming contention. I know that I am stronger for having the courage to step away from someone who did not respect themself and, therefore, would never respect me.

As much as I try and heal, in some ways, I am still being controlled by a narcissist who uses our kids to mess with my emotions and manipulate the situations that come up in our parenting plan. I still feel just as emotionally drained as I did when my relationship with Benny first started. Some things just do not change.

My journey is not over. As time went on, it became apparent that there were many coping mechanisms and bad habits I learned while I was in survival mode that kept me alive at the time, but now I do not need them. I have had to start to unlearn them because my future success depends on it. This takes time, and I am still actively in counseling for the effects of trauma.

I have been doing cognitive behavior therapy with my counselor in hopes of relearning healthy coping mechanisms and to sort out whatever anxiety I have left from my situation.

In October 2022, my divorce will have been final for four years. I have now been out of my abusive marriage for the same amount of time that I was in it, and I am still not whole. I have been working hard to rebuild empathy towards myself and recognize my own self-worth. I can tell you that trauma is not all in your head, as one might think sometimes. It is in your heart, your nerves, and your stomach.

I still have a very physical reaction whenever I have to see my abuser. I get triggered by my past, my breathing gets uneven, and my hands tremble. I go back to being on eggshells, and I cannot wait for the visitation time to be over. It is not just your mind that went through the trauma. Every cell in your body was there, and your body remembers it.

As time has passed, I have realized that the support of my family was the only reason I could make it as far as I have. I think back to how I started when I was at my lowest mentally. I had no job, or savings, literally owned nothing, was a college dropout, and had three little children who depended solely on me.

There were many, many times that I wanted to go back to my abuser, if only because I did not feel like I could do it on my own.

Thankfully, I had my family and did not have to do it alone. There was always someone around who could help me, whether helping me with my kids or giving me a pep talk when I lacked the confidence to keep putting the pieces of my life where they needed to be. I am almost certain that I would have gone back to Benny had I not had my family close by.

I know that other survivors are not as lucky to have had support as I am, and I do not take that for granted. I took things one day at a time, and I was able to figure things out. I started volunteering at Project DOVE to help others like me, and I went back to school as a single mom and graduated from college.

Most importantly, I made the sacrifices I needed to make to put my children first and to realize that if I allowed myself to be caught and thrown back into the boiling water, my kids were also then caught and thrown back into the water as well. I kept this in mind as I started dating and looked hard for the red flags in every man I talked to.

I have since met my Love After. The man that would come into my life after a classic, textbook experience with domestic violence and show me what love really is.

For a while, I kept making excuses for my children's father, thinking he did not have the time to see them. After I met Chad and I saw how much he did for me and how much he did for my children, I realized that just as Benny had chosen to be abusive, he had also chosen to abandon his kids as well.

I began to get some more perspective on the situation, and I could see that truly, actions speak louder than words. Chad and I have since gotten married, and I will not even begin to compare the two marriages because there are no comparisons. They are totally different experiences.

Together he and I are taking on the task of parallel parenting with a narcissist, which is no easy task and brings a lot of heartache. I tend to let my emotions get the best of me, and he can help me take the emotion out of the situation and look at the logic. He is incredibly patient with me as I learn that I do not have to apologize for everything and has shown me grace as I get used to being an equal partner in life for the first time.

I have members of my family that are reading this chapter in this book, and this is the first time that they are hearing any of this. I hope some things make more sense to them now.

Like the year that I missed my dad's birthday party and could not give anybody a good reason why. That was the same weekend I went to the shelter for the first time, and I did not dare leave because I did not know if Benny was looking for me, and I didn't feel like I could take that chance.

My siblings all used to ask me why dad was paying for my phone when I was married with kids. Dad paid for my phone because Benny had no plans to, and my dad wanted me to be able to have one. It was the only lifeline I had in the middle of all the isolation, and my dad knew it. I may not have been able to tell anyone what was going on, but at least you all knew I was alive when I texted back.

All I can say is that I was victimized. I was in a fight that was never a fair fight. It was a fight I did not want and did not ask for. I always wondered what you all thought of me during those years. I have had people ask me how I can be so happy after everything that has happened. It is easy to laugh it off and reply flippantly.

But I think the real answer is because I know I am a survivor, not a victim. It is a lot easier to stay silent about it and just move on. But I know that staying silent does not help other people.

Leaving an abusive situation is an empowering place to be if you choose to step up to the plate.

One thing I have learned is that when trauma occurs in your life, it always creates change. Usually, it is a change you did not choose, but it happened anyways. With trauma comes healing, and healing is creating a change that you did choose. That is what makes it empowering. There have been so many times when even though I had left, I still did not feel free. But at least I can look you in the eye and say that I am not a frog who was boiled to death.

Tasha Rae

Facebook: Tasha Rae @TashaRaeAuthor
Instagram: @Tasha.raee
YouTube: Tasha Rae

About the Author

Tasha is a 24-year-old trailblazer telling her story to help heal, inspire, and educate women. She has a background working in the psychology field with traumatic brain injury survivors and people who are experiencing brain cancer. She received her Bachelor of Science in psychology and a minor in sociology. She creates YouTube videos sharing her voice and knowledge that she has discovered along her journey. She has traveled around the world, loves the outdoors, painting, dancing, acting, and spending time with her friends and family.

She lives by: "It's never too late to do what you want to do and be who you want to be."

Faith over Fear

When your high school sweetheart turns into a collegiate nightmare. A 4 1/2 year rollercoaster that broke me piece by piece.

My story begins but ultimately ends with a chilling horror of reality, revealing how I went from a life full of energy and possibilities to a full-fledged living nightmare. I grew up always wishing for the best and seeing the positives and potential in all people. As a young girl, I remember daydreaming about what I wanted to be and who I wanted to be. I was full of life and energy. I wanted to be me and all that entailed regardless of societal expectations.

I grew up in a moderately conservative hometown. It was the kind of city where you went to high school with the same people you had known since you were six. I always knew I wanted to explore the world and what life had to offer outside of where I was raised. When I was younger, I did not have an ounce of fear, worry, or concern about what could go wrong. Growing up, my older brother always looked out for me. He taught me that no matter what age, gender, or environment that I was in, I was always capable of anything I set my mind to.

My parents inspired us to have worldly views and experiences from an early age. It allowed us to see a larger perspective than the hometown viewpoints we were exposed to. They took us to new places and taught us about different cultures. They always encouraged us to try new things even if we didn't know how to do something. They were confident that we could learn and embody a holistic perspective. From a young age, my mom and grandma always lifted me up and supported me in not being confined by gender stereotypes. My mom always used to say I came out making a statement, and I couldn't agree with her more. I was outgoing, determined, independent, and always willing to try my best.

Embracing my carefree nature, I grew up dancing and performing. Dancing felt so freeing and soul-fulfilling. I was open and ready to try many dance areas, such as tap, ballet, jazz, hip-hop, and Scottish Highland dancing. When I was six, Scottish Highland dancing felt right for me. I went on to dance and compete for ten years. My dance teacher was a major influence in my life, always encouraging me to believe in myself, stay consistent, and illuminate the importance of my artistic abilities. Through dance, I learned to be brave, face my fears, and that reaching my goals was more than possible. My childhood was full of spending time with family, learning about life, and having exciting adventures.

As life moved on, I attended a large high school with 1,300 students. It was a big adjustment for me, transitioning from going to school with the same people most of my life to a whole new environment. At this stage in my life, I was 16. I had spent two years on the dance team and moved on to a new journey on the cheer team. This meant I was going to cheer practice before and after school, taking college prep classes, doing hours of homework, and performing at multiple games a week.

I was starting my junior year of high school, which was known to be one of the most stressful years. I began to feel the burden of the pressure weighing down on me. I had the intense reality of exploring which direction I wanted to go in life and, most importantly, who I wanted to become.

Expectations were creeping in from teachers and society to pick a college major at a young age. When I was 16, every decision, no matter how big or small, felt like my world. My whole focus was learning to be a teenager, figuring out myself, and having first-time experiences.

At that age, I thought I had it all figured out. I grew up watching romantic fairytale movies and daydreaming of my prince charming. I would always imagine what a serious relationship would be like. My idea of love at that age was finding my soulmate.

I wanted to find the person that would respect me, hold my heart, take care of it, be honest with me, and make me feel safe and valued. I don't regret having high expectations. I didn't want mixed signals, cheating, lying, or having my heart broken. I always thought to myself that if he wasn't the one for me, then it would be a waste of my time.

When you're vulnerable with someone, I had assumed that it would be reciprocal, but my high school crushes had proven otherwise. Students at my high school were focused on having fun and being serious later. Yet, I felt ashamed that I wanted something serious at that stage in my life.

Many of the guys in my hometown had the mentality that it was time to move on to college. Life is short, so don't take anything serious, including relationships. I, on the other hand, had always wanted something more serious. Those around me were making excuses for boys and their toxic behavior, therefore, blaming it on young girls for having valuable boundaries and knowing what they wanted in a relationship. In other words, being respected and equal was not the norm.

I quickly began to realize the misogyny, sexism, and toxic masculinity that was all around me, in school, in adults, in communities, in sports, media; it was everywhere, whether people realized it or not. Gender for me was not a limit nor a definition of who I could be or what I could do.

As young girls, we were shown the societal expectations in media, schools, and sports that we "needed" to compete with each other—comparing each other, questioning: who looks the best? Who is the smartest? Who is the guy going to choose? Is she better than me?

It's soul-crushing and heartbreaking that so many young girls are taught that they should be anything other than themselves for the approval and acceptance of a boy. This turns into internalized misogyny. Imagine the love and power in respecting one another, being there for each other, and erasing the need the "compete" or receive any sort of imaginary "approval "or "acceptance" of a man.

You are worthy and valuable, just as you are. You never ever needed approval or acceptance because it is feeding into the insecurity of a man's "masculinity" in the eyes of society. Self-serving intentions with unjust expectations are just plain inequitable.

Here is where my journey began, slowly and painfully accelerating into a turbulent 4 ½ year rollercoaster of my life. During my junior year of high school, I became close with the classmates that I had grown up around. In these friend groups, I was comfortable spending time with my guy friends.

Likewise, my girlfriends were also close with them, and we would all hang out together, which included going to games, going on adventures, and figuring out life as teenagers. This was the year I was going to take school seriously to get my college prerequisites in order. Many of my friends at the time were also taking college prep classes, and in turn, we ended up having several classes together.

I specifically remember when I first got close to my abuser. He was close friends with my friends. As a result of knowing them for many years, I trusted them at the time. Through all of our memories and awkward growing phases, we had been there for each other.

I remember the day my abuser decided to sit next to me in class. From that day, it was like we were instantly connected. We could talk for hours about every topic, and even more remarkable was the fact that he also had every interest I had. We had so many similarities growing up. Such as living in the same area, going to the same lake, and participating in the same activities, all before we had even known each other.

At this phase in my life, I wasn't focused on wanting a relationship. In fact, I had always said I would wait until I met my future husband, maybe in college, maybe later.

I don't even want to think about that until I'm 30! It had become a joke in my family because I didn't want something "that wasn't the real deal."

Towards the end of my junior year, we became very close. As a matter of fact, we began hanging out all summer. During my senior year, I had many big life decisions to make; where I would go to college, what city, and what state. It was all becoming real to me how much bigger the world would seem after growing up in a place that was familiar all my life.

When school started that last year of high school, I had many classes with the same friends. Naturally, he was in one of mine again, and he would walk me to class. He began to buy me snacks and coffee, and above all, he was always there to listen. I began to feel safe with him, and that meant I finally felt seen. He was putting so much energy into getting to know me as a person, and this was a level of effort that I wasn't used to in high school.

All of my friends would hang out with him. He got good grades, loved playing sports, and ultimately seemed like a good guy to me. He would always make me laugh and listen to me talk about hard moments in my life.

He would consistently text me to see how I was or to just check in with me.

At first, I was not interested in him. It was like he was doing all the "right" things, so I didn't question it. I was excited to have a good guy friend that was always there for me. Before I knew it, our relationship began to feel like a blur. I went from not knowing this person very well to deep conversations and to him longing to know every detail about me.

As senior year went on, we became extremely close, texting daily, calling, facetiming, going to lunch, going on hikes, bowling, and going to the movies. There wasn't a day at the end of senior year when I didn't talk to him. He began leaving notes on my car, notes on my locker, buying me flowers, writing vulnerable letters, giving me gifts, and asking me to prom in the most elaborate way.

Because of the way he made me feel, I began to have feelings for him. He would call me the most beautiful girl in the world and open up about his struggles in life. I told him all of my deepest vulnerabilities in every way. He would tell me about his past relationships and how they always left him, cheated on him, or would "turn" on him.

He made it so easy to feel empathy for him. I had experienced similar things in my past, which led to an instant connection for me to bond with him.

As a 17 year, old, I had never felt this before. I thought this was love, right? This person did everything to make me feel safe and heard. I was falling in love, or at least at the time, what I had thought was love. A major decision was hanging over us. Before senior graduation, we had to decide where we would be going to college. At the time, I had gotten into my dream college. I had always dreamt of moving somewhere new, being able to meet new people, and having new experiences.

He had also been accepted into the same college as me. I remember being so excited to share a new journey and chapter together. I had gone from not wanting a relationship to wanting to share a life with someone. A dramatic shift that I could not even see in myself yet. I was 17 and thought I was falling in love. So naturally, I was confused to hear him say he wanted to go to a different college in a different state.

That broke my heart, and I didn't understand. His actions and words had said differently.

I wanted to fully support his decision no matter what college he picked. However, that didn't mean it didn't hurt that he didn't choose the same one. After graduation, we continued to spend the summer hanging out together with our friends.

At that time, I felt subtle shifts happening. He started not to text me as frequently. He would tell me one thing, and later I found out it was something different. I began to feel confused because everything he had shown me before didn't align with his actions. I would make small excuses for him in my head.

I gave him the benefit of the doubt for lying to me over what seemed like little things because every moment and every action leading up until then had seemed so different. Before he left for college, he wrote me many letters, with dates on them and when to open them. I thought this was so sweet and thoughtful at the time.

Many were in deep detail, and they seemed like they were written from a romantic movie. This kept me romanticizing what our future could be and what it would feel like. We both agreed we wanted to explore where this relationship was going.

As the last of my high school summer was up, I remember the first moment where my whole body froze, where life didn't feel real. It was the night before I was leaving for college in a new state. I was laying in my bed trying to anxiously fall asleep with the thought of moving somewhere brand new.

I remember getting a text from him telling me he had kissed another girl at a party and that he didn't know what happened.

Thoughts began to swirl in my head as I convinced myself that this wasn't real; it had to be fake. He had just joined a fraternity, and I assumed it was a prank. I tried coming up with any reason in my head why this isn't real. He then proceeded to call me crying, having the biggest breakdown. Sobbing in his fraternity backyard and needing other people to go calm him down.

I later found out he had made out with another girl, along with getting numbers, snapchatting, and having deep emotional talks with girls that I had never heard of. Most of all, he was telling people he was single when he clearly wasn't. At this moment in time, this hurtful reality is something I found out about much later. He proceeded to call one of my girlfriends at the time, needing to "talk it out."

It seemed as though I was the one being cheated on, and it somehow turned into me needing to feel bad for him. Somehow the night twisted into me being the one needing to apologize for not "understanding." Right then and there, my trust shattered, and my perception of him, me, and this relationship changed.
The trust that he had spent so much effort on building in the months leading up to this very moment was gone.

I remember spending all night sobbing and feeling numb, not knowing how to feel. I remember sitting in the car the next day reading paragraphs of texts from him apologizing and "explaining" his behavior. Begging me to forgive him and vowing that this would never happen again. After arriving at my new out-of-state college, life somehow continued to move on. I had so much on my plate to figure out that I kept moving forward.

My first few months of freshman year were the beginning of my relationship straight from hell. The unforeseen cycle had started. We were continuing a long-distance relationship that required trust, honesty, and communication. I had trusted him with my life before that moment. He had a way with words, elaborate texts, letters, facetime, and phone calls.

Even going as far as sending me flowers and gifts in the mail and planning trips to see me.

He was full force love bombing me yet again. His tactic of showering me with romantic words and gestures had left me with complicated emotions. See, his caring disposition had another side, as there were moments where I would see his anger seep through his mask.

Anytime I mentioned my concerns or brought up the night he cheated, he would blow up on me for expressing the pain he caused me. He would say things such as, I couldn't just "move on" or "let it go." It came to my attention that anytime I brought up how I was feeling and wanted to talk about how he had been treating me, it would turn into something much darker. It was all fine and beautiful until it wasn't. When it was bad, it was dangerously bad. This cycle had left me on a hook, wondering where did that loving person go.

Is it because of the long distance? Is it because of me? Was there a possibility that he was right? Ultimately, I began to question the reality of things and myself. I had never done that before, as I had always trusted my intuition and myself. I was taught to trust my instinct and believe in myself and my value. Why was I questioning myself?

In time, I would start to see suspicious signs. Such as people on social media sharing moments that he had spent time with that I had never even heard of. It was like we were together but living in two different worlds. I remember feeling as though he showed me a side that no one else saw, so that meant he loved me, right?

One of the biggest red flags is acting one way to you and the complete opposite to others. I had taken it as he showed me his true self, which turned out to be dark and twisted. I started to feel uneasy when moments of his "true self" came out, but it wasn't someone I recognized.

However, this was easy for him to keep his mask on as I would only visit him on the weekends for two to three days at a time. At this stage in my life, I was juggling going to school, joining a sorority, working, making new friends, and trying to balance a long-distance relationship all throughout my freshman year of college. This made the perfect recipe that plunged me further and further into his web of torture.

As soon as sophomore year rolled around, his lies and deceit had caught up to him. A text from a girl that I had somewhat known through high school peers popped up on his phone.

I was very confused because I didn't know they were close, as she was also his best friend's ex-girlfriend at the time. He had never talked to me about her before, and I had no idea that they were "close" in any way.

This was after almost two years of dating. She would later be weaponized against me, just like the other girls he had used to threaten me with before her. He immediately deleted all the messages and blew up on me, screaming and cursing me out. I was sick to my stomach and knew he was hiding something by the way he was reacting. Naturally a narcissist's favorite tactic.

I messaged her wanting to know the truth for once, wanting someone to just be honest with me. I then found out they had been calling and texting for our entire relationship. He was consistently emotionally investing in her life, giving her advice, confiding in her about intimate and personal details, talking to her about me, and continuing to smear my name.

She was coming to him for relationship advice and emotionally investing in him as well. Isn't this what you call an intimate relationship? I couldn't believe the "truth." It left me feeling numb inside.

I had never heard of this girl before, and she explained that they were extremely close. There were text messages of flirting between them.

He went on to threaten that he was going to have sex with her, call her, and text her. In time, he would eventually continuously unfollow and follow her back on social media. He followed that same pattern with every girl he had ever been with or dated. I remember wanting to throw up, feeling like I had been emotionally violated like he had made empty promises. He proceeded to call me crazy and controlling for wanting to know the truth.

I sat in the cold, freezing October air for an hour that night, wanting to leave my body. It was like the night before college all over again. The night he begged and promised this would never happen again. I was tired of being lied to by him, by his friends, and by girls that I didn't even know.

I deserved respect and honesty. I felt like I had continuously been stabbed and left on a stage lined with prison bars in the center of his friends, his family, our hometown, and his fraternity and secretly ridiculed and humiliated. All I know is that if I had ever been in a situation where I knew something, I would never hide it from someone.

Providing the truth about someone's behavior can save others from a future filled with mental and physical abuse and even possibly dying at the hands of another person. A future that was almost mine. My mind was again in a fog, and mass confusion was swirling around my brain.

My ingrained belief about trust at the time was to always believe in the honesty of people and that people can change. He spent all of his energy convincing me that this other girl meant nothing. I was who he wanted to be with, and they were "just friends." He kept repeating the idea that he was not raised that way. Somehow life moved on throughout the complicated chaos.

A few short weeks later, I became very ill, which turned into frequent visits to the emergency room. I was diagnosed with chronic tonsillitis. It was as though right when I would feel healed, I would become gravely sick again. The weight of the world was coming down on my shoulders while I was away from my family and my "friends" from the past were no longer in my life. I felt as though I was alone, grasping onto the hope that everything would work out.

When Thanksgiving came around, he continued feeding me stories of what our life could be like in the same city.

It seemed as though he wanted to show me that he was committed and that he wanted me to be a part of the life that he had created there. At this point, we had been together for almost two years, and I felt that moving closer would help our relationship. If we were in the same place, it would be like before. Everything would go back to being amazing like it was in the very beginning.

Before making a final decision, we had many deep conversations about me making a move to be closer to him. Within a week of deciding, I visited him and toured apartments close to his fraternity. We eventually decided on one down the street from him. It finally seemed like we were going to be on the same page again.

However, when winter break came around, I needed surgery to remove my tonsils. I had become very ill, and they were poisoning my body. After I had surgery, I felt so frail and weak.

The day after my surgery, which was a hell of a recovery as a 19-year-old, he brought me a milkshake and was supposed to stay with me per the doctor's recommendations as there were many health concerns. I was in so much pain and wanted to feel supported and comforted by my boyfriend.

Someone I thought could be there for me in a scary time. After all, we had been together for nearly two years.

Nevertheless, he stayed just one hour and had already made plans with friends. He then criticized me for not having people come to visit me. Then he turned me into a living homework assignment by naming off things that I didn't have as a 19-year-old. Despite the fact that I was really sick, he began listing off everything I wasn't and everything he thought I needed to work on.

All the while, I was laying in my bed in extreme pain, trying to recover. He wasn't there for me in the way I thought someone who said they loved me should be. This was barely two weeks before I was supposed to pick up my whole life and move to an apartment in a different city. I felt trapped because I had already signed a lease just down the street from him.

At that point, my life was completely isolated, away from all my family and friends. I remembered the extreme hurtfulness from the mental and emotional abuse he inflicted on me. It caused me to throw up, I was unable to eat, and all the while trying to heal from surgery simultaneously. In a little over a week, I had lost 20 pounds.

It became clear that when he was back in our hometown, he was a totally different person. In reality, I was seeing the person he was all along. The facade he was upholding had begun to show itself to me. I remember feeling so trapped and confused. I didn't know what was real and what was a lie in his life.

No one in my life knew the extent of the abuse he had been slowly inflicting upon me. I don't think I fully understood or wanted to even admit it myself. I thought I still had no choice but to move, especially after signing a lease. I convinced myself that no matter what, I was going to go and persevere to create a new life for myself. If I could do that the first time I went to college, I knew I could do it now.

Somehow, I made it through the two weeks left of winter break, and the time finally came for me to move to a new city. When moving day arrived, my family helped me set up my new studio apartment. He came over maybe once to see my new apartment but never cared to help me move or to see how I was doing.

Once I had gotten everything set up and figured out, my family left. There I was in a 300-square-foot studio that he could see from his fraternity. I was in a new city with no friends, a new school, and no family and recovering after losing 20 pounds from emotional pain and a difficult surgery.

Reality set in quickly, and little did I know what my life was about to become. As time passed, he was texting, calling, and wanting to hang out all the time. He had told everyone that we had broken up, but I wasn't aware of that lie until later. This is the place where the truth started to reveal itself.

See, he had fabricated a picture of his life in his fraternity, located in his college city, where he could create a life he wanted to depict. Everything I knew before was gone. Everything about my life was his. He began to come over whenever he wanted, and if I wasn't responding when he expected me to, he would wait outside my apartment and bang on my door until I let him in.

Eventually, he had a key to my apartment, and now he had access to me whenever he wanted. He began to leave his belongings at my apartment, stay whenever I was out of town, and eat my groceries. This continuously gave him a reason or a *need* to come over.

At this point in my life, I was going to school full time and trying to survive as a college student. So, by no means could I afford someone leaching off everything I owned. At that moment, I thought it was because we were playing house. His being there all the time was as if we were living together.

As time went on, I was so excited to become closer to his friends and start building a life there. I wanted to have a new friend group and feel at home. I began to notice and feel as though when I was around them that they knew things I didn't. They would mention many details about my life that were meant to be between him and me.

I was always just the "girlfriend" to them, though. Not Tasha. Not me being my own person and wanting to get to know them. I began to realize that they would make jokes about me being crazy. It clicked in my brain that he had planted the seed months ago to make me the crazy girl. The controlling girl. The girl whose image he created to discredit anything I could say about what was really going on. This was his perfect poison. To say cruel things behind my back so that if I told anyone what he had been doing to me, they would write it off.

I slowly realized the reason why he had treated me so badly right before moving there. The truth was, he didn't want me to see the reality of the lies he had fed people. The facade he had worked so hard to keep was already in place. He loved to play the victim and intentionally manipulate the narrative to fit his personal public image. To him, his reputation was everything, even if his truth was so different behind closed doors.

Consequently, I fell into a depression because moving to a new city with the "love of your life" was much different in my head than when I got there. He had successfully isolated me, love bombed me, and made himself the only access point for my life. Every single thing in my life was through him now.

Conversations now turned into repeated episodes of hitting me, punching me, choking me, ripping my hair out, slapping me, throwing things at me, repeatedly breaking my belongings, threatening me, holding weapons at me, and kicking me across the room.

There wasn't a swear word or derogatory term that he didn't call me. I was told to drink bleach and to kill myself. He began to devalue everything and anything about me.

My appearance, what I wore, what I ate, my weight, my hair, the pictures I posted, and the people I talked to. He also tracked every guy friend I had ever had and any communication with.

I often had to hide the messages I had sent randomly, trying to reach out to my friends, hoping they would believe me and listen to me. During this time, I didn't have the courage to tell anyone the full truth. He would go through my phone while I was sleeping and log into my accounts. For him, nothing was off limits. He would test me by making fake accounts and texting me on fake numbers to see how I would respond.

If I didn't do something he wanted, he would get violently angry. He would go on a social media rampage, liking girls' pictures, following them, messaging, flirting, snap chatting, threatening to ask other girls on dates, or sending texts to his exes. My life was being controlled by intense fear. I was deeply scared to even admit it to myself. Admitting the truth to myself was admitting the things he had been doing to me. I wasn't ready for that yet.

The darkest night of my life – and the ultimate truth- is it is etched into my brain forever. I will never forget the pain, the sounds, the words, and the actions.

I don't even remember how this "argument" started that night. I think it was because I said I wanted to hear the truth about his actions or that I didn't believe his denials about something he really did do.

Being with someone who continually covers up their actions gets very exhausting. My intuition had been screaming at me, and I couldn't ignore it anymore. He was sitting in the chair next to my bed, facing me and cussing me out. He told me I was always too emotional, never let anything go, and called me every single name you could think of.

I got to a point where I couldn't take it anymore and screamed for him to "please just leave, just leave me alone." Until then, I hadn't had the courage to stand up to what he had been doing to me out of fear of what could happen to me. He refused to leave my apartment and became extremely angry.

When I made it to the door, he attacked me, violently kicking me in the stomach, clear across the floor. He saw my phone in my hand and realized I was going to call the police and escape his rage. He then proceeded to break my furniture and threaten to harm me. I kept screaming for him to leave as I was shaking in fear.

He pushed me onto my bed, ripping the canopy off my ceiling and holding my neck and chest down with all his weight.

I was stuck between wanting to black out and feeling numb inside. He looked me dead in my eyes, grabbed my kitchen knife, pointed it at me, and told me, "You better shut the fuck up or else." After being abused for the past several hours, I remember feeling like I was leaving my body and finally accepting he was going to stab me and kill me.

I will never forget the moment I looked death in the face and accepted that I was never going to walk out of that studio apartment ever again. He was grinning and viciously laughing in the satisfaction that he had threatened to kill me. His glossed-over black eyes looked dead inside.

My survival instincts kicked in, and I began to watch everything I said at that moment. I had to walk this fine line to survive. I acted as though things were better and tried to pretend and make him believe that I forgave him. Knowing damn well, my soul was trying with every ounce to survive this moment. I knew I couldn't let him take my soul.

Once he had set the knife down, he grabbed my phone, computer, keys, and wallet, leaving my apartment for an hour or two. Time felt like it lasted forever and yet stood still all at the same time. I later found out he was sitting outside on my apartment stairs, lingering around to make sure I couldn't tell anyone or get help.

Once he finally left, I felt so much pain physically, emotionally, and mentally. I laid on my bathroom floor, locking the door and sobbing, not wanting to be alive. I wanted to die and wanted this to be a bad dream that I could wake up from. I begged God to end my life and to take me away. I had never felt so drained and violated in my life. I felt worthless, like I didn't matter, and at this point in my life, I didn't think anyone would care or notice if I had died.

His isolation tactics had worked. This was the only way out I saw at the time. From the depths of despair, I made it through that night. Slowly, I found I was living in a fog, and the cycle started over again, only each time, it came more frequently. Fear at this point was deeply entrenched in my mind, body, and soul. Over time I was being abused every single day. Some days it was sexual and physical abuse.

However, in reality, it was constant abuse depending on the day; it just would be in a different form.

Even when it was the "beginning" of the cycle, it was still mental and emotional abuse as his actions were never with good intent. There were many times when I wouldn't get out of my bed for days. There were several moments like this that caused me to live in a constant state of fear, fatigue, and being anxious about every sound I would hear. I began to scream and jump with fear whenever something caught me off guard.

When moments like this would happen, he would cool down as if a switch had flipped. He would act as though everything was normal, which led to him profusely apologizing and sometimes even apologizing a few days later or denying that it had happened altogether. Thus, continuing the love bombing all over again, trying to entice me back in and change my narrative of what really happened.

Anytime he had suspected me pulling away, planning to leave, or telling someone, he would either react in anger, abuse or love bomb me. It had begun to feel like a complicated and confusing prison. It felt like my soul had been broken, and my life was continuously sucked out of me.

I began to see everything in the world as scary and harmful.

As my junior year of college came around, I began to really question my life, who I had become, and where my life was going. I began to think of myself for the first time, what life could look like after college, and where I would want to go. Our relationship, or what was left of it, had fallen into a continual abusive cycle. I had gotten used to continuously hiding every blow-up he would have on me, every mark, every bruise, and every time he would verbally, mentally, and emotionally abuse me.

When springtime came, I was finally ready to do something for myself. I began volunteering and shadowing in the rehabilitation department with traumatic brain injury survivors at one of the best hospitals in the country. I shifted my focus to the study of psychology. I had a deep sense and desire to understand everything about the brain, emotions, trauma, and how I could help make an impact in this world. I wanted to feel like I could matter and that my life meant something. This was when I began to feel a shift.

Secretly feeling like I could relate to people who had survived immense traumas and witness how incredible they grew from that experience in so many ways.

I was also learning from an amazing team of women in the psychology field who always supported me in my growth. They will forever have a place in my heart. Without them knowing, they helped me believe in myself, gain confidence, and trust my knowledge and skills.

We talked about women in medicine and the path that they had carved for me and younger women. I finally felt like I had a place in this world outside of the hell that was my life at the time. I knew I wasn't going to let him destroy me.

July of that summer was when I reached my breaking point. It was late at night when he had blown up on me and abused me again. I remember calling my mom, sobbing, and finally telling her a tiny piece of the truth about some things that happened that night. I told her about the things he had said but still wasn't able to tell her the truth about the physical abuse just yet.

At this point, I had made one friend who I had become close with. Since I was away from family and support, my mom encouraged me to call her and tell her. At this moment, I knew I was making a choice I couldn't come back from. Accepting it myself, saying it out loud, and finally telling a friend what had happened to me that night was terrifying.

I was finally starting to realize what I was in and realized I needed to get out safely. I facetimed her and confided in her. She was instantly there to support me and secretly help me. I felt like I could finally be believed and heard for the first time.

Just as soon as senior year began, I was finally ready to pick myself up and secretly make a plan to leave and ultimately save myself. Before this point, I had tried to pack a bag and escape many times. I would always get roped back in because he would text my friends and family saying he was "concerned" and hadn't talked to me in two days. It was easy to make my family concerned living so far away. When in reality, he knew exactly what he was doing and wanted to pull everyone I knew into his chaos to control me.

He would threaten to post explicit photos of me, harm me or people in my life, and the list goes on. When it came to moments like that, I would have rather taken the abuse myself than allowed him to hurt anyone in my life. It got so far to the point that year that when I was visiting my family for Thanksgiving, he showed up screaming and knocking on the door for an hour, incessant calls, sending multiple texts to me and my family, along with ruining pies and cards that I had made for his family.

He was starting to unravel his true identity to everyone in my life. This is when I found out his parents were aware of his behaviors and assured me that he would calm down and that it would be ok. They were adding to the cycle that continues in their family. It was apparent I would have to get out of this on my own.

I made a plan to get a job, support myself, make it to graduation, and get the hell out. My friend, her boyfriend, and their group of friends had secretly become aware of what had been going on. This helped me to continue to strive forward in the darkest moments of my life.

Somedays, I didn't think that I had an ounce of energy left, but I knew I couldn't give up, that I deserved to live, and that I deserved better. At the beginning of 2020, the pandemic had just begun when spring break came around. I found it as an opportunity to find some space and get out of this huge city to go visit my friend's family.

During this time, colleges were shutting down, along with fraternities and sororities closing. My abuser decided to go to his hometown for spring break.

When visiting my friend and her family, I decided to open up about things he had done to me. Her whole family and her boyfriend's family had sat me down and validated everything that had happened to me. Letting me know that I was supported and deserved to get out and leave.

This made it clear that people believed me and that I would be heard and seen for the truth in the chaos he had created. The day after I got back, I decided I was done with being abused, done with him, and done with this relationship. I was going to pick faith over fear.

I was done living in a consuming whirlwind of fear, hurt, and pain. I was going to have faith in the complete unknown and that every single thing about my life was going to change. I was tired of being outcasted by people calling me crazy, not believing me, and living an intricate lie. I no longer cared what anyone was going to say or do. I was choosing to save my life.

I had secretly been collecting years of evidence, including documentation of my injuries, his threats, and abuse of all forms. So, I knew, without any doubt, that I could show and ultimately prove the truth of what he had done to me.

Meanwhile, he was in another city at this time, and I knew with the pandemic that it was my saving grace. I texted him and told him I was done, and it was over. It was the only way that was safe for me to tell him.

I also broke down and told my family how serious it really was. Subsequently came the weeks of hundreds of texts, calls, and messages on every single social media platform possible. He also sent threatening texts to my friends and family. After leaving him, he would constantly go on "runs" by my apartment.

I knew he was trying to spy on me in any way possible. His scheming and grasping at any form of manipulation were in full force for months. In fact, he did not tell a single soul for over two months that we had officially broken up and that I had left him. In the past, he had always been able to manipulate me into coming back, but this time I held firm. He was unable to persuade me to return to the abuse.

He wrote explicit texts to my family and me stating he knew what he did and that HE didn't want to go to jail, lose HIS job, HIS future, HIS friends, or family over HIS actions.

I moved in with friends right away, who helped to look out for me and keep me safe. Even after moving a little farther away for a second time, he would be seen jogging down the street.

I made a plan with everyone in my life that I wasn't going to be alone during this time. I have since moved three times. I didn't get a restraining order at the time because it would legally keep him posted with my current address and any future changes, which completely defeated the purpose.

At that point, I had never been so exhausted. I was finishing college, moving, and having panic attacks daily. I was struggling to find resources that could help support me and to get a specialized therapist who understood abusive relationships. I was constantly being turned away and told that I wasn't a priority if I wasn't in immediate danger.

When I could get help, it would take a month or two to even get an appointment. I finally had the courage to tell my doctor. He helped me get connected with social workers and therapists the next day. That is when I was diagnosed with post-traumatic stress disorder. I had severe nightmares every night, constant anxiety, lost weight, lost handfuls of hair, and was dealing with the stalking, and fake accounts, even after I had blocked him on everything possible.

I had spent months scream crying every single night because this was when I had to come to terms with every little thing that happened to me. I had to accept that this relationship was a complete lie, that I was broken piece by piece, manipulated, and used for everything I had. I felt like a shell of a human. At night, there is no hiding and facing the reality of it all. My mind and body didn't know how to relax and feel safe going to sleep. I had been living in survival mode for several years, and I had forgotten how to exist without abuse.

Most importantly, I was finally choosing myself and learning to balance work, a new life, and healing. It was difficult to relate to anyone my age. My life had been flipped upside down, and I had no idea what was coming next. I felt like I had wasted years of my life. Most days, I felt as if I was a hundred years old. It took a long time to forgive myself and to forgive what had happened to me.

Some days I would feel better and feel that anything could be possible. On other days I would see the same type of car he had, a specific color of a t-shirt, a song, or something someone would say, such as a specific phrase, and my body would be triggered into a panic.

I recognized and came to terms with knowing that my healing journey isn't linear. I was learning to love myself for the first time in a while and to give my mind, body, and soul the grace that I deserved. I realized nothing has power over me unless I give it the power.

As more people found out, the more I realized who was a true friend and who wasn't. I remember feeling this passion and fire in my soul to speak my truth. I was mixed with anger, frustration, and pain. Pain in what I had been through, pain in what I continued to have to struggle with, and pain in not feeling heard and believed. It took several months after I left to express the full truth of what I went through.

Even after admitting I had been in an abusive relationship, there were many things that I couldn't tell anyone. This book is helping me to express things that I haven't told anyone besides a few close people in my life. In 2021, I felt compelled to speak up. I made a YouTube video sharing my truth. Even though many people did believe me, many still gossiped and criticized me. No one will truly ever know the hell I had to crawl myself out of alone.

That is a feeling survivors will never forget. The strength and courage it takes to pick yourself even in the darkest moments of your life is incomparable. After sharing my truth, so many amazing survivors began to reach out to me and speak more openly about their truths, even beginning to express this in their own lives. Through this healing journey, I held onto the conviction that if this could help even one person out there, everything I went through would be worth it.

Throughout these challenging years of attending school, I summoned up every ounce of strength and graduated from college. It was one thing I refused to give up on. At times, it was my mental break from reality, and I knew it would be an accomplishment no one could ever take away from me.

I went on to move to a new city, giving me the gift of a brand-new beginning in a place where people could meet Tasha for Tasha. A future filled with people who would be meeting who I am now, in essence, my "new" self, the person who is free from having anyone or anything weighing me down. It is a place where people could get to know me, not through someone else and not through my abuser. It is the beginning I had wished for, for years. To finally feel free, to finally experience a feeling of peace and belonging.

I decided to try new things, go to new places, and meet new people. It felt like I was a kid again. I began working in the field of oncology neurology, hiking, going out, taking acting classes, and posting videos. I found my soul friends who help me grow, encourage me to believe in myself, and always support me in everything I do.

I can finally fully accept myself, embrace faith in the unknown, and have faith in myself and in the world. I no longer let the fear of him finding me, wanting to hurt me, or smear my name affect me. I realized the people who are ready to see the truth will and the ones who don't aren't meant to be in my life.

Challenging the beliefs that people had for so long challenges the views they have of themselves and their lives. It is a beautiful lesson not to take it personally as we are all on our own unique journeys that only we can see and experience. Even in the darkest moments of my journey, I knew that this was my road to uncover and that everyone battles their own challenges.

I recall the moment I decided to tell my truth and how scared and discouraged I was. I had sent a message to his mom telling her everything that had happened to me and asking her if she wanted to see pictures and videos of my documented injuries.

I never heard a response back. They continuously tried to cover it up and act like it never happened.

That is something as a survivor I had to accept, never hearing or receiving the recognition of what happened to me. This was something I learned to validate for myself. Because no apology or action would ever alleviate or help the pain and destruction that was caused to me and to my loved ones.

I learned to turn my pain into purpose and my experience into wisdom to help others, ultimately learning to give myself compassion and acceptance for who I am at my core. I chose faith over fear. Since then, I have never looked back. I knew that chapter of my life had come and gone. I gained a new version of myself. She knows how to turn her pain into power, her darkness into light, and her experiences into wisdom.

Living through and experiencing all that I have at such a young age, I can honestly say that I would not be who I am right now; the girl who is full of strength, fearless determination, and even hope for the future. I can assure you that you are not alone and will never be alone in your pain.

I am sharing my story to empower you; a beautiful soul who always deserves to be heard, understood, and above all to be seen.

Facebook: You Empowered Me/ @YouEmpoweredMe
Instagram: You Empowered Me
Tik Tok: @sandiegovictoria

About the Author

Victoria lives in sunny San Diego, California, with her two rescue dogs. Victoria fell in love with helping others, taking a career in healthcare. When tragedy erupted, Victoria realized her passion was not only helping others in healthcare but helping victims become survivors. Victoria has been a guest on several podcasts to spread the word about domestic violence. Her ultimate goal is to change the way our legal system treats survivors. When she is not working, she spends her time painting, cooking, shopping for crystals, or enjoying her time with her women's group.

You Didn't Break Me - You Empowered Me

When you feel the universe is against you but soon realize the universe is only making you stronger, powerful, and unstoppable.

If you had asked me what I wanted in life, I would have told you I had it. I had a loving husband who was always by my side, two adorable rescue dogs, a home I owned, and a great career. Of course, I wanted more, like children, a larger home with a wrap-around porch and an even greater career. But at that very moment, I was content with my life.

I met my abuser in 2014, on Valentine's Day, through an online dating app. Dating online was a nightmare, and I was ready to give up until I received a very lengthy message.

He wrote beautifully, telling me I was like no other woman on this site. I was educated, had a good career, poised and gorgeous. I remember reading that message over and over, really thinking that I either had another crazy person on my hands or my prince charming was finally found.

For the next couple of days, we texted all day and even spoke on the phone. He sounded handsome and charming, but I was worried I would find another dud. It was Valentine's Day, and I received a text. "This is my last time reaching out to you. I will be at Spacebar café at 7:00 pm. I would love to meet you. If you don't show up, I won't be texting you anymore." I hated that I was given an ultimatum, but I went anyway.

I wasn't physically attracted to him. He was shorter than I thought and spoke with a slight lisp. While we walked on the beach, he told me about his past. Growing up as a kid was rough. His mom fell into drugs when her mother passed away. She soon became a dealer, and in due time, her three boys became her helpers.

His father and mother would fight, throwing fists and eventually more. He would frequent his time at the library, sitting and reading for hours.

Soon his father found another woman and left him and his brothers behind at a young age, which devastated him.

As the years went on and he became older, he started selling drugs himself. When you're involved in drugs, other crimes follow shortly after. He was in and out of jail and landed himself in prison. He had finally decided to stop this lifestyle, and as soon as he was released, he went into programs to start bettering his life.

Let me start by stating that my life was structured. The only crime I was ever involved in was stealing my friend Lisa Frank's folder in the 2nd grade. I grew up knowing to stay away from people like him, and I took pride that I never was a troublemaker. So, when he was staring at me, waiting for a reaction, I panicked and said ok. My brain was telling me to run, but my heart was saying give him a chance, so I did.

We hung out every single day after that, and each day was better and better. After two weeks, I knew, that someday, he would be my husband. I knew at that very moment that I loved him, and he loved me. As the months went on, we introduced each other to our families, and we all bonded very quickly.

He quickly became my world, and I could not imagine my life without him. Years went by, and we were now living together. I adopted a dog, Marley, who soon became our world. Life was amazing, adventurous, and becoming the fairy tale I had always dreamed of.

One day, we were talking, and he asked me what my fears were? I told him that my biggest fears were being alone in the dark, fire, and strangulation. I know those were really over-the-top responses. But I live in California, where we have forest fires. I've seen my friends' homes go up in flames.

I also watch a lot of murder documentaries, and I can tell you now that nothing good happens in the dark. Strangulation has always felt so personal to me, and such a horrible way to pass. I asked him the same question, and he always responded that he didn't really fear anything but disliked worms. I laughed, thinking my fears were over the top while he feared almost nothing.

It was now 2016, and marriage was heavily on my mind. All my friends were married and starting families. With everyone around me having the life I wanted, I pressured him a lot. I knew someday, and someday soon, I wanted to call him my husband, so what was he waiting for?

I approached him but really got no response. Soon after, he asked if we could talk. He stated he felt like before marriage our focus needed to be on buying a home. Rent was getting pretty high, and he was right. But I was brought up that marriage occurred first before buying a home, so I declined his suggestion.

Days later, he confronted me and told me that if I didn't buy a home first, he was never going to marry me. I was floored. How dare he give me an ultimatum yet again and on something so major? I remember sitting in my car crying, thinking there was no way I would purchase a home with a boyfriend.

Why? Why would I do such a dumb thing? What if we broke up? What if he never proposed after? Am I stuck with him then? So many thoughts, questions, and worries ran through my head. Four months later, we were signing documents for our first home together, a cute 896 sq ft condo.

One evening, my abuser wanted to get intimate, and I was all for it. Intimacy with him was fantastic, and I often felt euphoric. But this time went differently. I have never been fond of anal intimacy, NEVER. The thought of someone hanging around my backside never intrigued me.

While kissing, he turned me around and ran his hands down my back. I knew immediately what he wanted, so I tried turning around, but he insisted. While he inserted, I cried. I begged him not to, but he didn't listen. As he pushed my face into the pillow, I cried, hoping it would stop soon. As his body fell next to me, I slid off the bed and ran to the bathroom, hiding my face. I was mortified. I couldn't believe I cried during the whole thing, and he didn't stop.

Did my "stop" mean nothing to him? When your woman is crying underneath you, you don't stop to ensure she is, ok? I realized then that I would have to be stern and tell him I did not like it. I walked back to the bedroom, laid down next to him, and told him my peace. No reaction; none. No sorry, no sympathy, not a care in the world. I let it go like I always did.

We finally got engaged on 12.05.2017 in front of our friends. It was magical, and I was ready to finally get married.

We decided our wedding date would be 01.19.2019. My fiancé wanted no part in the wedding planning. He expressed that he could care less and would just show up when he had to. This always bugged me because I wanted him to be equally as excited as I was.

I thought the wedding was going to be magical. I was hoping I would walk down the aisle to a sappy man, but that was not the case. The night before, he had made it very clear that he was not here to marry me but to see his friends and family. He sternly told me that he would stand in front of everyone and marry me, but after we said I do, I needed not to bother him and let him spend his time with his friends and family. I was mortified. While I spent every waking minute trying to coordinate a beautiful wedding, my groom asked me not to spend time with him on our wedding night.

One thing I wanted was to write our own vows. Watching other couples getting married and reading each other's personal vows always felt a little more special. When my day came, personal vows were a must! On the day of our wedding, I could not write my vows.

I was pissed and trying not to let anyone know our conversation the night before. I struggled with my vows. How could I write beautiful things to this man who wanted nothing to do with me? As the time got closer, I took snippets from google and made them my vows; pathetic, I know.

As I approached the hall internally, I was telling myself to run. Don't get married to someone who doesn't want to spend this incredible day with you. A day you worked so hard to make magical. Run, run far away, and don't turn back. But instead, I walked down that aisle, read vows from google, and married the man that wanted nothing to do with me.

I tried very hard to be happy. I danced with friends, thanked everyone for coming, and played this façade that I was blessed to be married. During the entire reception, I saw my husband twice. He hung out at the bar, disappeared a couple of times, and refused to be near me any chance I walked over. No garter toss or bouquet toss was done. The first dance was cut short, and any time I was approached by someone asking why I wasn't with my husband, I played dumb every time.

As the end of the night approached, I was exhausted, and all I wanted to do was take my dress off and go to bed. I asked multiple times if my husband was ready to go, and I was blown off every time. Every time, until his brother told him to take me back to the room. We walked down to the cabin in the dark with no light whatsoever.

He helped me take my dress off and then told me to get in the shower. We didn't have any towels, so he offered to go back up to get towels and come back. I stayed in the shower, hoping he would return, and we would have a romantic moment, finally together as husband and wife. Minutes went by, and he hadn't returned. I turned the shower off and used the blanket on the bed as a towel.

I realized I didn't have my clothes because they were in my mom's cabin, so I lay naked, wrapped in the small blanket. Twenty minutes went by, and he still wasn't back. I couldn't call anyone because I had no cell service, so I laid on the bed, still wrapped in the blanket, hoping he would return soon.

As minutes turned into hours, tears fell down my face. I was spending my wedding night alone, scared, naked, and cold. I spent a year making this night magical to end up alone in a room I was terrified to be in.

I closed my eyes and fell asleep, but then there was a bang on the door. It was my bridesmaid asking if I was ok.

No, I was not ok. I needed my husband, and he was nowhere to be found. She told me he was partying with his friends and would tell him I was looking for him. Hours went by before he came back. He undressed as I lay in the bed and fell asleep next to me.

No apology was ever given. He didn't care that he left me. He didn't care that my face was swollen from crying. He didn't care that my world felt rattled. It was a new day, and I needed to move on.

* * *

One week later, I got a knock on our front door, and my mother-in-law appeared with all her crap. She packed all her belongings and decided she would live with us. I was never told about this because I would have never agreed.

As she moved her bullshit in, I went to the neighbor's house to cool off. There was no way this lady was going to stay with us. We were newlyweds, living in an 896 sq foot home with two big dogs. We were already cramped. I called my husband but got no answer.

As I sat at my friend's house, my phone was blowing up with texts from her.

She demanded I come back to make her lunch and help get her things into the house. I ignored her, which was a bad decision.

When I returned to the house, my husband was home, along with his brother and mom. My husband asked me to come upstairs to talk. He instantly started screaming at me, telling me I was wrong and asking how I could treat his mom that way. It was apparent she told him her side of the story and that was all he was worried about.

I asked him why his mom was there, and it felt like he knew she would be there all along but did not want to inform me. As the yelling continued downstairs, I was mortified that my husband was acting the way he was. He yelled things like: I hate you, you're useless, I don't love you, you're a fucking bitch, etc. while his mom and brother just stood there watching.

He grabbed me by the arm and pushed me out the front door, yelling at me to find a new place to live. That house was equally mine, and there was no way I would leave without a fight. I pounded on that door for a long time, hoping he would eventually let me back in. While crying uncontrollably and banging on the screen door, the neighbors started coming outside and complaining, so I left and ended up staying with my parents for the night.

The next morning, I decided to go back home, hoping his mom and brother were gone and we could sit down and talk. The closer I got to home, the more of a stomach ache I got. I knew there wasn't going to be flowers and an apology when I got there, so why was I rushing home? I never understood why I was so eager to go back.

As I approached the front door, his brother came around the corner. I really didn't want to talk to him, but he stopped me from going in. He apologized for his brother's behavior. He agreed his brother handled things poorly and wanted me to know that he had a "heart to heart" with him. His final words before letting me in were, " You are the best thing that has happened to my brother. Please don't let this ruin things between you two."

As I walked in, his mom and him were sitting on the couch, talking and acting like it was another day in sunny San Diego. I walked past them, went upstairs, and closed the bedroom door. He immediately came upstairs and sternly told me I was in the wrong. He went on to let me know that if I behaved like that again, things would get worse than the night before. I felt like I was the prisoner, and he was the warden.

He just kept talking, never letting me speak, and explaining what was going to happen moving forward. His mom was going to stay, I needed to behave, and if I didn't, there would be consequences. Yet again, I stayed quiet and behaved like any good wife would do.

It was a little over a week later when his mom informed me that she was moving to Mexico. All I could think of was, "great, can you take your son?" It was amazing to see her get the hell out of my home. Hasta Luego!

We were fighting a lot more, and our one-year wedding anniversary was approaching. I thought a mini vacation would be perfect to mend our relationship, so I booked a trip to a small woodsy town and surprised him. As we drove down the driveway, a cute little cabin appeared behind the trees. It was quaint, with a claw bathtub, a huge fireplace, and a jacuzzi in the backyard. It was perfect, and I was hoping romance was on the horizon.

The first couple of days there were amazing. We hiked, walked the town, and he even decided he wanted to get a tattoo at the local parlor.

I wasn't happy at first because he wanted to get my name across his heart and include our anniversary date, but there was no convincing him not to. As he lay there on the table, holding my hand, he looked over at me with a smile; while I was nervous since something like this was so permanent.

The last day of the trip, I booked a tram ride in Palm Springs, about an hour away. The tram took you from the base of the mountain, with 100-degree weather to the top of the mountain, with below 20-degree weather, within two minutes. I was scared since we would be so high up, but I knew with him by my side, I would be ok.

As we waited for our tram to arrive, we argued about which door we should stand at. Since I was hesitant to go to the door he wanted, he threw a fit and raised his voice at me, surrounded by others. This was the first time he had yelled at me in public, and I was not happy. As we entered the tram, he came back down from his anger, wrapped his arm around me, and came back to the man I knew and loved.

We had a fabulous time up at the top. We took pictures of the great views, hiked a bit, and then decided to go back down the mountain and home.

We had not been successful at making a fire, and he was determined to make one. Before heading home, we stopped and gathered the supplies, which included items to make smores. As he proceeded to make a fire, my anxiety started going up. I hated fire, especially large raging fires.

As I said before, I have seen enough of my friends' homes burned to the ground due to forest fires, so fires were never good. I proceeded into the room to take a breather and remind myself that everything would be ok. As I sat and talked myself out of my anxiety, he walked in, holding a plate full of cake.

He approached me and said "What the fuck are you doing in here? Are you going to be a pussy tonight? Do you need to call your mommy, like you always do?" I sat on the edge of the bed with my head down.

He had never talked to me like this. Why would he say these things? I slowly lifted my head, tears billowing in my eyes, and said "Why would you say this? I am just taking a minute to myself. You don't need to be so mean." Right before I could turn around to look at him, he threw the cake at the back of my head.

Rage poured through me. How dare he do this? I instantly got up, turned to him, and told him to fuck off. Instead, he egged it on more. He proceeded to continuously call me a pussy. As I pushed past him and entered the kitchen, I saw the rest of the wedding cake on the counter. He was behind me, belittling and reassuring me that I was the biggest fucking pussy.

I couldn't take it anymore, so I grabbed the rest of the cake and threw it at him. As the cake flew through the air, it hit his back, bounced off of him, and landed on the ground. As soon as it hit the ground, resentment went through me. How could I stoop to his level? Why would I do something that I hated him for doing? I grabbed towels and the trash can and immediately started picking it up.

He went into the bedroom, came out, walked right past me, and out the door. I cried the entire time while cleaning up the cake. My tears were for multiple reasons, one being I couldn't enjoy the cake I waited a year to try and two, I can't believe my husband and I fought the way we did. Are we going to recover from this?

It took me nearly an hour to clean since the cake had got into the grout of the pretty wood floor.

As soon as I finished, I went into the bathroom, cleaned myself up, and then went back to the living room to watch some T.V. I realized I did not have my phone on me, so I got up and started searching for it, but I could not find it, along with my keys and wallet. He must have taken my things with him. What the fuck?

I was terrified of being alone in the cabin and was hoping my husband would return so we could talk. Hours went by, and finally, headlights filled the house up. He was home. He struggled to open the door, so I got up, unlocked the door, and laid back on the couch. He walked in, not saying a word, and stood right in front of me.

What was going on? He just stood there staring at me, waiting for me to look up at him. As soon as I looked, he started removing his belt and said, "The next time you disobey me, things will get worse. For now, I am going to whip you into submission."

As soon as his belt was off, he whipped the belt across my face. I froze, wondering what was going on. He whipped his belt over and over, across my face and the right side of my body. I had no idea what to do, so I sat there and took it. I looked forward watching I love Lucy play on T.V. while each whip stung my body.

He wasn't stopping, and the whips were becoming more painful, so I got up and ran into the spare room. He followed. I knew he had my phone, so I dropped to my knees and started feeling his pockets. While I searched his body for my phone, he grabbed my arms and tightened his hold. "Ouch, you're hurting me," I screamed. "Where is my phone? Give me my phone back!"

He tightened his grip even more and said "I didn't take your fucking phone. Are you going to call your mommy, you pussy?" As he tightened his grip, I noticed my arms start to turn purple, so my instinct was to bite him and bite him hard. He let go and screamed.

As I tried to get up, he pulled me up. He pushed me onto the bed, got on top of me, and put his arms around my neck. I realized that all three of my fears happened on that day. I panicked and struggled to get him off me. I remember I looked behind me and noticed that I was close to the window, so I started pounding on it, hoping the neighbor would hear. Nothing.

As I struggled, he choked me harder. His stare was filled with such evil. It was almost like my husband was no longer inside his body. The struggle felt like a lifetime. I kicked and wiggled my body, hoping he would release me, and he finally did.

I immediately got up and ran outside, noticing that he was not chasing after me.

My throat hurt, but I knew I had to scream and scream for my life. As I ran down the driveway, screaming HELP, I noticed that the neighbor's house had their lights on. I ran towards the lights, hoping someone would be able to help me. As I inched closer, I noticed a man in the kitchen window, so I threw my hands up to the window, startling him and begging him to call 911.

The door opened, and an older man walked out. I collapsed on his stairs and begged him "Please call 911. My husband just strangled me." His wife ran to the door and guided me into the house. As I sat on their couch, I realized the man had gone outside to look for my husband while his wife handed me a glass of water and a wet washcloth. She hugged me and continued telling me everything would be alright. But it wouldn't.

My life was turned upside down, and I knew things would not get better. The man walked back inside and said, "He appears to have driven off. You are ok now. Do you need anything?"

I replied, "Please sir, call 911."

All I could do was cry, but I was so panicked that I couldn't even catch my breath, so I was hyperventilating more than anything.

He asked me a couple of times if I truly wanted 911 to be called. He informed me that if 911 was called, he would go to jail. Of course, I wanted him in jail! Why would I want otherwise?!? So, he proceeded to call 911. As we sat and waited, the couple gave me their phone, so I could call my family.

One hour later, a young, short sheriff arrives. He had this "better than now" attitude and asked what had happened. As I sat and tried to understand what happened, he interrupted me and asked "Did you egg him on? Were you guys doing drugs? Did you drink tonight?" These questions lit a fire under my ass. How dare he walk in here and ask that?! So, I respond, "No. Does it look like I do drugs? I've never touched drugs in my life. And no, I wasn't drinking but if I was, would that justify this?"

As the officer stared at me, he told me my husband would be going to jail. As much as I wanted him to go to jail, my voice told the officer, "No." I was more afraid that if he went to jail, my life would be in more harm. I begged the officer to let him go, even though I knew he needed to be arrested. The officer ignored me.

Minutes later, both officers came back to the house. "So, your husband is headed to jail. It appears he made dinner, took a shower, and was asleep when we walked in. We need to take some pictures before we leave." What the actual hell!? He ate dinner, took a shower, and went to bed? All while I was there, in some stranger's house, trying to grasp what just happened.

The officer asked me to proceed to my house. So, I got up and walked out. As I entered the house, the sheriff asked me to take my clothes off. I didn't understand why I needed to get naked and, better yet, get naked in front of a male officer. But I was extremely tired and had no energy left in me to argue. I stripped down to nothing. He took photos as I stood in the middle of the living room with no clothes on. I was mortified. I felt even more violated and more alone than ever. As he finished with the photos, I ran to the other room and got dressed.

I wanted to talk to my husband. The officer led me back down the driveway to his patrol car, where my husband sat in nothing but his boxers. "What the hell? How could you do such a thing? Why would you hurt me?"

He looked up, stared at me, and then at the officer and said "Who the hell is she? Why am I sitting here? Let me out. I was sleeping, causing no harm. I came up here alone. Why am I being arrested?"

Sheer frustration came out of me. Thank God I respected the law because if I didn't, I would have broken through those bars and beat the crap out of him. The officers proceeded to ask me again if I had seen him do drugs and or drink tonight.

This time, I could not say no. It felt like he was on something. The man sitting in the back of the car did not act like the person I had known for seven years. I informed the officers that I did not see him take anything.

As they drove off, I realized I would be alone in this house with no phone. There was no way I could sleep, so I cleaned. I knew it would be my last night here, and my parents were arriving in the morning. So, I packed all of our belongings and cleaned the house so I would be ready to leave the moment they arrived.

While packing, I heard a ring. As I searched the house, I found his work phone. On the line was a collect call from the jail. I stupidly answered it.

He immediately screamed at me, telling me I needed to get him out and that I was ruining any future for him moving forward. He kept reminding me that he was an ex-felon, and there was no way they would let him out without me coming forward, stating it was all a lie.

Instead of feeling sympathetic, I asked him for the location of my belongings. He didn't want to give me the location and continued to use profanity, so I hung up. He called 23 more times. I didn't even know a jail would allow so many calls.

The next morning, as my mom packed my things into the car, my dad broke into the truck to search for my missing belongings. He was able to find my wallet, keys, and phone under the driver's seat. He also found a bag full of empty whiskey bottles with a receipt, confirming he bought those when he left the house for a couple of hours.

I contemplated calling his mother to let her know her son was in jail. I wanted her to know since I was leaving and not returning up here to retrieve him. As the phone rang, my gut started turning into knots. As she picked up, I told her why he was in jail.

Her response was, "What, did you do to egg him on? You made a vow through sickness and health, so you better go pick him up." I couldn't believe the words that were coming out of her mouth. I always knew something was not right about her and this conversation justified her true evilness.

As we gathered into the cars and got ready to head home, I got a call from a bail bonds. They told me that I needed to pick him up from jail, that I had bonded him out. HOW?! I never called a bail bonds, and I never agreed to bail him out. I was completely shocked and extremely tired, so I picked him up.

We had a 2.5-hour drive home, and it was completely silent. I could not believe I had driven him home. He never apologized. Instead, he just sat there and looked out the window the entire time.

I drove separately on the way to court. As a friend and I sat in the parking lot, he blasted an Eminem song called "Farewell." Moments before, he had posted the song to his Facebook account and hinted to me to listen to it. The lyrics are evil and talk about shoving the woman into an oven and feeling the gratitude of choking her. I like Eminem, but he has become evil, and his songs prove it.

While he stared directly at me in the courthouse parking lot, he put on his blazer and proceeded into the courthouse. Not even minutes later, I got a notice that the case had been dismissed due to a lack of evidence. My shot at justification was over, and there was no way to fight it.

I don't know why I thought life would get better because it didn't. When I returned to work, I had panic attacks so bad that my director took me to the local women's shelter for help. I waited eight hours for the lady to tell me they could not help. I was numb and knew I would never be ok.

I stayed in the same house with him for six months. During that time, my life became hell. He once told me he would get help, but he never did. He would stay home during the day and be gone through the night. He would occasionally come home and break through the window since coming through the front door was not an option (exaggeration).

During this time, he would threaten me, occasionally chasing me around the house with our kitchen knives. He would demand sex, telling me that it was my duty in this world and what a wife should do.

When I refused, he would force me to give him oral and then rape me.

He refused to have vaginal intercourse with me, so it was always anal. He would push my head into the pillow and penetrate me as hard as he could, sometimes leaving me bloody. I was now his punching bag. Along with the rapes and knives, he would remind me of his gun, taking pictures of his gun in his mouth and letting me know that he would use the gun if he needed to.

Twice, he pushed me out of the car while on the freeway because he was "over me." While I walked home, he would slowly drive behind me, yelling slanders out the window.

I was always angry with him but never had the courage to leave him.

One morning, I was cleaning the house and found a pipe. It looked like a crack pipe and had a white substance in the bowl. I knew it was drugs, and I was pissed. It was equally my house, and drugs were not going to be stored there. I texted him, told him not to come back home, and that he was not welcomed there anymore.

In the early morning hours, while I was asleep upstairs, he broke into the house again. I wasn't going to keep quiet; I was pissed.

I started yelling at him and told him to take his things and not return. I walked into our second room, which was my work office, and started logging into work. He walked in and started throwing my belongings at the back of my head. I turned around, infuriated, and started screaming at him to get out. That only made him more upset.

He started picking up bigger items and chucking them against the wall, letting things shatter across the floor. I pushed past him and down the stairs, but he followed. As I sat on the couch, he opened the large air vent and proceeded to take large gallon-size bags of white substance out and put them into a backpack. One by one, large bags of drugs left my air vents. He pulled out a spoon, foil, and a lighter and placed it on the coffee table in front of me.

"Before I leave, my last request is to drug my wife." There was no way I was going to get drugged. If he didn't think I put up enough of a fight before, he was in for a rude awakening. We argued back and forth, and as I walked away to call 911, he grabbed my arm. I pulled hard and made him lose his bearings. I immediately called 911 and asked for help.

Two officers arrived, and I informed them that he had threatened my life again and had a backpack filled with drugs. They told me to go upstairs, sit on my bed and wait for them to call me down. Our bedroom window was right above our backyard, so I could hear the whole conversation. The sheriffs treated him like he was their friend. My abuser informed them that he was moving, and I wasn't allowing him to pack his things.

The officers told him to grab all his stuff and put it on the backyard patio. They informed him that he was no longer allowed in the house. They were going to lock him out, but he would have access to the backyard.

As he piled stuff into the yard, I noticed he was not taking his things; he was taking mine. So, I opened the door and yelled to the sheriffs. The male officer came upstairs and, after hearing me out, told me that he could take whatever he wanted; they were just belongings.

He packed my jackets, shirts, underwear, and anything else he wanted. The officers asked me to stand in the corner while he proceeded to take my pillows, blanket, and sheets from my bed.

I was pissed. They locked the slider door and asked me to come downstairs.

As I sat on the stairs, my abuser was outside, taunting me. The officers advised that I should file a restraining order and move out. I informed them that I owned the home. I asked if I could change the locks since my abuser informed them that he was moving. The male officer laughed and told me I could not change the locks because he was co-owner of the home and that was illegal. I felt like the officers did not care about me and were 100% on my abuser's side. I called my mom, and we proceeded to her house with my dogs.

As I sat in her house, trying to figure out what I would do next, I got an alert on my phone- our bank account was wiped clean. He had gone to the bank and withdrew all of our money. I screamed and then broke down in tears. He had taken every single dime out of my bank account and left me with nothing.

In a rage, I told my mom I wanted to get a U-Haul and move out today! She agreed. So we got in the car, rented a U-Haul, and went to my house to start packing my things. When I got to the house, I was determined to pack everything but his shit.

I hired movers on short notice to pack my furniture and help me move out faster since I was afraid he would come home. As I drove off, I felt invigorated. I just spent the last 2 hours blindly packing everything I could. I was done, and it felt amazing.

The next morning, I found a storage unit and started moving everything from the U-Haul into the unit. I decided I needed to return to the condo and grab some more things, so my family and I headed back. I noticed the door was wide open, and the neighbors were hanging out front, which was unusual. I hesitated to go in, but the neighbors told me no one was inside.

As I got closer, I could smell a foul odor. As I stepped in, I noticed food everywhere! He had taken the items from the refrigerator and thrown them all over the first floor of the condo. There were beans and soup dripping from the ceiling, raw meat laying openly on the floor and counters, and every condiment squirted all over the floors. He had ripped some of the drawers and cupboards off the hinges. The house was a mess.

I walked upstairs to find even more of a mess. Anything I had left behind was destroyed. Pictures of us ripped up and thrown, shattered glass all over the carpet.

My desk that I left behind had been hit with a hammer. Clearly, he was pissed that I had moved and found it appropriate to destroy anything I had left behind.

All I wanted to do was leave, but my mom insisted on cleaning everything up. So, we stayed and cleaned the entire house. If I was not sure yesterday, I was sure today that my life with my husband was officially over.

Six days later, after the San Diego riots were over, I was able to walk into the courthouse and file a restraining order. I was numb and felt like a victim the moment I walked into the room. I spent most of the day waiting for my temporary court order to be approved.

The final thing to do was serve him and wait for our hearing. Serving him was a nightmare. He was nowhere to be found, so I struggled to serve him. Days later, my parents got a knock on their door. A large, tall man came up and asked for me. My parents told him I was not home, but he sat out front arguing with them and told them he wouldn't leave until I showed my face. I would not let someone threaten my family, so I walked outside. He walked up, looked me dead in the face, threw the paper in my hands, and told me, "You've been served." I've been what? What the fuck?

As I sat down and looked at the papers, I cried yet again. How could *he* serve *me*? I read his complaints. He told the courts that I bit him, threatened him with a knife, and took his money and dogs. Right then, I knew I needed a lawyer, and I needed one fast.

After six court appearances, *six* of which he failed to appear, I was finally granted my restraining order. His restraining order was dropped for not showing up. I felt relieved. Would this be the start of my new life?

I lived with my family while I dealt with all of this. I slept on the living room floor with my dogs. It was hard. I never had a moment alone where I could cry and try and understand what was happening with my life.

I wouldn't describe my family as horrible people, but they tend to release frustration out on me. I have always been the punching bag in the family, and it always made me resent them. Some of the names I was called was satans spawn, bitch, freeloader, and the list went on. I was beaten down during my time there, and it was exhausting.

After many days of torment, I was removed from the home and told to find somewhere else to go. If I thought I had already hit rock bottom, I was wrong. At that time, I was working from home. So, my office was either at a friend's house or sitting in front of Starbucks. Once I was off of work, I would call around to shelters and see if they would help, but I was always turned away, mainly due to COVID-19.

I am grateful for my friends who allowed me to stay in their homes, but it didn't change the fact that I was homeless, broken, and ready to end my life. I spent weekends driving up to the mountains and contemplated taking my own life. What did I have to lose? I would sit there for hours, strategizing how I would do it, usually thinking about driving off the cliff.

One day, as I was parked in front of a cliff, I heard my grandfather. My grandpa passed in 2018. He was my world and truly the only man in my life that treated me like I was a human and someone to be proud of. He cherished me, and I cherished him back. As I grappled with my life, I heard him tell me to stop. He told me to turn around and face my reality. Find God. Find happiness because it was there. I just didn't want to see it. So, I got in my car, onto the highway, and headed back to reality.

I spent every day after that working hard to get my own place. I wanted my dogs back, who were still at my parents' house. I wanted a house where my dogs and I could live comfortably, with no anger and turmoil. Five months later, I was able to get an apartment and move my girls in.

It was so rewarding to finally have a home where I didn't have anger as soon as I walked in. I didn't have to tend to anyone. I didn't have to clean the house when told; I could just live the way I wanted to live. I still felt scared being in a place alone. Even though I had my two dogs, and they would bark at any noise, I was still terrified. I ended up buying a gun, leaving it close to my bedside, and it made me feel safer than ever.

Every day since I left, I have received a call from an upset neighbor, detective, lawyer, sheriff, district attorney, you name it, I've heard from them. Since leaving, my ex-husband has been involved in some serious crimes. He has been on the news for several of them. His first crime was running into a busy street, trying to hit as many fire hydrants as he could.

Weeks later, he drove his massive truck into the second-story indoor mall.

He drove through one end and out the other end of the mall, waited for cops to arrive, and then received a ticket and was let go. He has stolen vehicles, committed robberies, vandalism, sold drugs, etc. The list just got worse as the days went on.

Since his crimes occurred during COVID-19, he was never arrested and booked. He was simply ticketed and let go until now. Now he is in jail and facing a short amount of time for just some of the felonies he has committed. It amazes me that the justice system condones the number of felonies he has committed in just a span of 2 years. He has harassed me and hacked into my phone, email, and social media accounts. Every time he does, law enforcement never does anything about it, even with a restraining order in place.

I have struggled to get our house sold. I was awarded the home with the stipulation that I would sell it and split the proceeds with my abuser. Since the day I moved out, he has allowed over 40 individuals to break into the house and move in. In the state of California, if someone breaks into your home and receives a piece of mail with that address on it, they are considered tenants and receive tenant rights.

With that being said, tenants have more rights than homeowners in California. I have gone to court numerous times to evict the current tenants. Once I evict, not even hours later, the next group breaks the door down and moves in, and I am stuck having to go through the entire process all over again.

Most of the tenants have had at least one felony conviction under their belt. They live in my home, destroy the property, and upset everyone around them. They have never paid a single dime in rent, at least not to me, who handles the mortgage. They have driven motorcycles into the house, used Dremel tools on the walls, and daily sold large amounts of drugs from within the home. I have been harassed by them, too, and do not feel very safe in my city.

In total, there have been over 300 phone calls to the local sheriff's station regarding the home. I have spent hours and every dime I had to remove them properly. I have had sheriffs tell me that they want no part in this, and others tell me they will help and then ghost me.

I have had every DA attorney approach me; every local detective tell me they are helping, and no one actually follows through.

I even approached our city supervisor, who wrote back, informing me the same thing I always hear, they can't help. I am now working with the local news stations, hoping they could assist with this.

Honestly, I have no faith. I'm tired, and I've come to terms with letting the house go into foreclosure, something I prided myself never to do. But as the years go on and the bills pile up, I am forced to move in that direction. Don't even get me started with our justice system. In my opinion, they are useless. I would have never said that before this journey. I always prided myself on being a law-abiding citizen who paid her taxes and lived a pretty normal and quiet life. I was the woman who would advocate for our sheriffs and always thought, "they did no wrong." I mean, on the side of our local police cars, it does quote, to protect and serve.

But after living this nightmare, my local law enforcement has not been there to protect me. They have only made matters worse. It is a shame that they would "serve and protect" the felon in this situation over the "no criminal record victim." Allowing myself to speak up for what is right has made me in control of the situation before me. As I still respect the law, I don't allow the law to treat me as a victim. I will find justice with or without their help.

As I struggled with getting help within my community, I randomly saw Stand Up Survivor on Facebook. I took a chance and reached out to them. I noticed they were having an upcoming retreat, and I knew I needed to go. Their team reached out to me, and I was invited to go to their retreat in Nashville. I had no money to go, but I knew I needed to be there.

After work every day, I worked for Uber Eats. They had a promotion going, and if I delivered 150 orders within two weeks, they would give me 1,300 dollars. So, after my full-time job, I set out, delivering food. It was exhausting and nerve-racking all at the same time. Here I was, scared of the world, afraid someone would attack me, just like my husband did, all so I could make enough money to go on this much-needed retreat. I was frightened, but the retreat was always in the back of my mind. I felt that if I did not get to have this opportunity, then what else do I have to look forward to?

I had never flown alone before. The flying part didn't scare me. It was more of trying to find my way around an airport with no help that scared me. As I walked into the San Diego airport, I reminded myself I needed to let the worries fly out the window and embrace what was yet to come.

I should be proud of myself for going on a plane and experiencing another state alone. How amazing that I even get the opportunity to do something like this. And I am so glad that I did.

I made incredible friends, and even after a year, we still catch up and see how things are going. It felt amazing to hear other women's stories and leave knowing you are not alone. We all had heartache, but we all showed tenacity, strength, and determination not to allow our abusers to win. It was the most humbling and gratifying experience I have ever been involved in.

If I could give any advice to any survivor, it would be to enroll in a domestic violence retreat. Give yourself the opportunity to open up and share what you have been through. Meet the other women who are also sharing the journey. Partake in every activity and put 100% of your focus into what you are doing every minute while you are there.

One thing the retreat had us do, was write a letter to ourselves. We were able to read it aloud, and then the ladies framed it for us to have. I have it up on my wall, and I read it daily.

I wrote:

Victoria,

Do you realize what you have endured? Not just in your marriage but in your family life, job, and even friendships? So much pain and heartbreak, but so much strength has been formed inside of you. You might want to go to the "dark side" but remind yourself that you have got this. Remind yourself that you're beautiful inside and out. You're worth it and ready to conquer anything that comes your way. Always remind yourself that **YOU** come first, and **YOU** make the decisions in your life. Don't beat yourself up. You will make mistakes, but you will soon blossom into a strong-willed, beautiful, and empowering woman. Remember, he didn't break you; he empowered you.

I stayed after the retreat to experience vacationing alone. It was extremely hard to do but also so invigorating. I had never taken an Uber, let alone by myself. I was terrified to get in the car with a complete stranger, but I overcame it. Walking the streets of a new town was scary, but I overcame it.

Meeting strangers was something I would never do alone, but I overcame it. It was the first time ever; I felt the chains fall off of me, and power surrounded me. I was 33 and finally becoming a woman.

When I returned home, I told myself I would face my fears. On the plane ride home, I wrote down my fears and made a plan that I would face anything I feared head-on and not allow it to stop me from living. Soon after, I hiked up to a peak in the dark with just a small headlamp. When I made it to the top, emotion ran through me. I made it, and now it was time to go back down three miles, completely in the dark. I was frightened, but my friends would not let me give up. I had no choice; in order to get to safety, I had to keep walking.

As I jumped in the car, reality came to me that I could do anything I put my mind to. I hiked in complete darkness, and I was so proud of myself. Since that hike, I have done an additional three hikes at night.

I can officially say that I can light a match without the fear of being burned. I can light a **BBQ** and not panic. I know it sounds so pathetic, but I faced it head-on! I can finally be around a fire and not be scared.

I was afraid to speak up when others put me down. I had allowed most individuals to walk all over me and dictate what my life should look like. I soon realized I was not living; I was just being. I spent weeks after the retreat writing down what I loved about myself and posting them on my mirror.

Now I am nowhere close to loving myself 100%, but allowing myself some room for internal love, allowed me to take back control of my life. I now dictate how my story will unfold. Taking back my power has allowed more doors to open and has allowed me to live my life to the fullest. I no longer fear speaking up for what is right. And I no longer allow others to write my story.

I entered myself into a contest where the winner received a boudoir shoot. I expressed how I was taking my power back and finally embracing life. I won and became the 2021 most empowering woman of the year shoot. I walked into that photo shoot, not loving who I was in my skin. Oftentimes people made fun of my weight, so feeling beautiful was a challenge for me.

As I walked through the doors of a beautiful downtown flat, I was embraced with confidence. The photoshoot made me feel fierce and empowered.

As I received the photos back, I realized that even with a big belly, fat thighs, and a double chin, I was still beautiful, still a human, and I was taking my power back.

Every day, I face more and more fears. Every time I do, I remind myself that I am unstoppable, powerful, and amazing. I often say the quote that has got me through everything, "He didn't break you, he empowered you."

My abuser is currently in jail, awaiting his sentencing. In October, I get to finally face him and read my impact statement. I have spent hours upon hours figuring out what I want to say to him.

Parts of my current statement reads:
"Today marks 881 days since I left. You would think after 881 days that I would be on my road to freedom and not standing in a courtroom giving a victim impact statement."

Towards the end of my statement, it reads, "Whatever you want to be called today, you are a heartless individual. You call yourself a man, but you're far from one. For months, you drilled in my head three steps.

You insisted that first, we sell the home, second, we divorce, and three, move the hell on, but you couldn't do that. You called me weak and told me I would amount to nothing. I am here today to tell you that I am no longer weak, frail, or naïve and that not *me*, but *you* will amount to nothing. I have become a strong individual and will not take anyone's **BS**. This won't be the last time you see me, but it will be the last time you ever see me in the flesh. I will be making a stand, fighting for justice, not only for me but for every other individual going through this same battle. Even though it's only for a short time, I hope you rot in your cell, and I pray that no other individual ever be hurt by you."

Oftentimes, women tell me how strong and brave I am. I never understand why because I am doing what any woman should do. But as I go through this journey, I realized more women keep quiet than speak up. I believe that if I remain silent, the cycle of abuse will never stop. What do I have to lose? My abuser has and continues to tell me that once he is out, he will find me and hurt me. So, I can either keep quiet until he does or be loud and make a change.

Even though I still endure hardships, I remind myself that I was put in this world to fight this battle. And not necessarily a battle for me but a battle for every abused woman out there. I will cry and feel like giving up, but I will stop and remind myself that I am powerful, strong, and successful. I will not let my abuser beat me down. I will not let my story be another tick on the abuse charts of no success. I will not stop and will work hard to help other women regain their power. I will remind myself and others daily, "He did not break you, he empowered you."

Photo by: Ostoff Photography

Kathy Wilson

Website: https://www.wilkjaneart.com/

About the Author

Kathy Wilson (she/they) was born and raised in New England and spent some time wandering around the Pacific Northwest before settling (at least for now) in the Upper Midwest. They love sea smoke sunrises over Lake Superior in the winter and hiking in every season with their partner and their dog. Kathy loves painting with bright colors and wearing outfits that include several different (possibly clashing) patterns at once. Learning to show up as her authentic self is the story of her survival. Relishing in the small joys of daily life is how she practices gratitude and cultivates hope.

When the Abuse Doesn't Leave Marks

*How I survived coercive control and
learned to trust myself*

I had just graduated from college, and the only thing I was sure of was that I wanted to experience places I had never been to before. I wanted to travel and relish the journey. I wanted to learn from people who were different from me and see landscapes I had only ever seen before in photos or movies. I wanted to stroll through a city with no destination or plan and just see who I met, where I ended up, and what I could learn. I wanted to eat foods I had never tasted. I was fascinated by how geography and climate influenced the culture of places, like their architecture and cuisine. I wanted to learn about the world, and I had to get away from home.

Growing up, I got the message that it was more important to appear okay than to actually be okay. Secrets were normal. It was all fine as long as no one found out and you looked normal from the outside. It wasn't just little white lies. It was big giant secrets. Like how I didn't find out I had another sibling, and they didn't know who one of their parents was until we were both almost 30 years old.

Manipulating others was normal. It was just a means to an end because there was no way any of us would be held accountable for our actions. Small mistakes were punished with harsh criticism and shaming. The sarcasm we exchanged was caustic; we used it both as a shield and as a weapon. Anger and disappointment were the only acceptable emotions to express, well, for men at least.

When I was little, my anger was laughed at. Once I turned thirteen, my anger was dismissed as bitchiness. If I cried, I was told I was only doing it to manipulate people. Vulnerability was synonymous with weakness, and I learned it should be avoided at all costs. Love was conditional. I learned to follow the rules because compliance was rewarded with praise and affection. I learned that it was more important to prioritize the needs and wants of others than to be true to myself and what I needed.

By age 22, I'd lived away at college in a different state for a few years. I had started to realize that many of the rules I'd learned growing up were written by someone who was desperately afraid of being authentic. They covered up anxieties and insecurities with a smokescreen of authoritarian control. I didn't want to end up like that, and I didn't belong there. I needed to find a place where I could grow without being pruned to fit into someone else's uninspiring garden. (As it turns out, I am actually more of a cute but sorta overgrown front garden, growing a combination of food and native plants).

I didn't know exactly what I was looking for, but I was optimistic that there was something better out there for me. So, I signed up to volunteer for AmeriCorps and headed off to Alaska. This was pretty much as far away as I could get from home without leaving the country. I sold or donated most of my stuff, packed a couple of backpacks and a tent, and got a one-way plane ticket to a place I'd never been before. I was assigned to a crew repairing trails on a remote island known for having the highest concentration of grizzly bears in the world and a larger population of bears than people.

A six-passenger float plane dropped us off at our worksite, where we lived for the week in our tents. They sent us out to the worksite with a toilet seat screwed onto a piece of plywood with a hole in it. We learned how to dig and build our own temporary pit toilet for the season. There was no electricity or running water. We hauled water from the lake to our camp and did all our cooking over gas camp stoves.

I learned how to manually cut down huge trees with a crosscut saw and how to make those trees into boardwalks winding through the perpetually soggy temperate rainforest. I heard bears rustling around in the woods foraging at night while trying to sleep in my tent. We made a point to talk or sing while we were out the trail so the bears could hear us coming and avoid us. Even though we knew the bears were all around us and we saw signs of them everywhere, we rarely saw the bears themselves.

The scariest animal encounter I had in the Alaskan wilderness was with the biggest beaver I had ever seen. I came upon the giant beaver in a clearing by a river's edge, littered with the creepy, jagged jawbones of spawning salmon. I was terrified sometimes, but I was also learning that I was capable of more than I had thought.

I arrived in Alaska as a clumsy, unsure nerd. But here I was, living in the wilderness, doing a physically demanding job, and surviving giant beaver encounters.

The AmeriCorps volunteer stipend was nowhere near enough to afford the cost of living in Alaska. So, on our days off, we were essentially homeless, and the trail crew would camp together or sometimes split the cost of hotel rooms. We'd go to a restaurant and determine if we could collectively afford something like five entrees for eight people. So, we'd just order that much and pass the plates around the table, taking bites until we'd finished all the food. We were often without phone service or a way to charge our phones, but we still always found each other. The material conditions weren't great, but it felt like freedom. We supported and relied on each other, and we became a family.

I was just starting to figure out who I was and who I might want to become. I was learning new ways of connecting and living in community with people. I was learning how to find and share the kinds of joy that existed outside of material possessions and capitalism. I was starting on my life's journey to understand myself and find my purpose.

That's when I met the man who would become my husband. Because I didn't have a home for those several months I was in the AmeriCorps program, I'd often spend my alone time reading or journaling in public places. I'd go to the library and coffee shops during the day and restaurant bars in the evenings. A bar at a restaurant was usually much quieter than a regular bar, and I was much less likely to get hit on by drunk men (although that still happened).

One evening I had finished my dinner, and I was sitting at the bar settling into a good book when a man sat down next to me. After a bit, he started to make conversation with me. Normally when a dude started a conversation with me while I was sitting at a bar reading, he would remark on how interesting it was that I was reading at the bar and then quickly switch to trying to flirt.

These types of men really thought I was sitting at the bar reading as some kind of signal that I must be looking for attention. It was so impossible to get it through their heads that I actually just wanted a place to sit and read that I often had to get up and move to the other end of the bar or just leave.

A lot of the local bartenders recognized me and checked in to make sure I was okay if it looked like a guy was bugging me.

This guy was different. He seemed to understand that I was there to read, and after a couple of questions about what I was reading, he left me alone. It wasn't until I put down my book and was getting ready to leave that he asked me if I'd like to stay for a drink with him. Drinks and conversation led to more drinks, more conversations, some hikes, and within a couple of weeks, we were dating.

He was a good-looking guy. Okay, he was really hot. He was over six feet tall and had a very muscular build. He didn't judge me for living in a tent and hotels because he lived on a boat. He had a nerdy biologist job that sometimes took him out to remote wilderness locations for several days at a time, so he thought it was really cool that I was on a trail crew. He was 11 years older than me, but it felt like we wanted the same things out of life.

Every day we had off work together, we'd go out into the wilderness. We hiked thousands of feet up mountains to absolutely stunning views of the islands and mountains of Southeast Alaska. We went kayaking while bald eagles flew around above us.

We camped on the beach and watched orca and humpback whales swimming out in the cove. We walked out on a frozen glacial lake. We climbed through surreal blue ice tunnels in the glacial icebergs that had been floating there when the lake froze.

I loved that he loved being outside as much as I did. And I loved that he accepted me and what I was doing with my life without judgment. A relationship with him felt, at first, like the better life I had wanted when I left home.

I had no plans after my AmeriCorps service ended, and I was dating this great guy, so I decided to stay in Alaska and look for a job. After two months of dating, we moved in with each other. I needed a place to live, and it was easier to afford to split the rent between two people.

Even though we were living together, we barely saw each other during the first year we were dating. We only had one day off a week together. He worked days while I worked evenings. He would be asleep when I got home and leave for work before I woke up. Sometimes he'd come home on his lunch break, and we'd talk while I ate breakfast and he ate his lunch. But there were stretches of days where we didn't talk and only saw each other asleep.

About four months after we started dating, he told me his job was sending him to a backcountry camp for a month to collect data and samples. He had me drive him to the small, local airport to help his coworkers pack up their supplies for the trip. I saw him walk over and start helping them before I left.

I had no reason to believe he was lying, so when he got upset that I asked how to contact him in case of an emergency, I was caught off guard. Finally, he told me I could call the main line at his work but not to call it unless it was an absolute emergency. Otherwise, his work would get annoyed, which could reflect badly on him.

When I asked what happened if I needed to call outside of normal business hours, he said I wouldn't need to and started to get upset until I dropped it. The day he left, he only took an empty backpack, saying that all the gear and supplies he needed would be provided by work. He wouldn't let me drive him and insisted he was getting a ride from a coworker. I told my coworkers, friends, and family that my cool boyfriend was off in the woods for a month doing nerdy biology stuff, and that was that.

Until a few months later, when my coworker, who had been open that their boyfriend had to spend some time in jail for a DUI, mentioned that our boyfriends knew each other from when "they served their consequences together." I didn't quite understand what they meant, but I just nodded along. When I got home from work that day, I turned into a super sleuth online and found out that my boyfriend had gotten a DUI while we were dating and had hidden it from me. Then, he pretended to be on a work trip when in reality, he was serving time in jail.

Growing up, I learned that when people were embarrassed or ashamed, they tried to cover it up with lies. It's more important to appear okay than to be okay. Now that I had an adult relationship, it was my job to make it look happy from the outside, no matter what was going on inside.

He had made me an unknowing accomplice in his lie, and I felt ashamed, even though I didn't know I was lying for him. I was worried it would reflect badly on me if people found out about it, so I felt I now had to keep this secret for him. When I confronted him about lying to me, he got upset with me.

He said that I was being sneaky and that it was a violation of his privacy that I had found out about his lies.

A few weeks later, he wasn't there when I came home from work. When I woke up the next day, he still wasn't home and wasn't answering his phone. So, I started calling local hospitals and then the jail. I found out he was picked up for public intoxication and being held until he called someone for a ride or sobered up. I was upset that he was so willing to cling to the possibility that he could lie about this and get away with it. He was willing to sit in a holding cell for almost a day while I worried about where he was instead of calling me for a ride.

That was the last straw. When he got home, I broke up with him before he even had a chance to make up a lie about where he had been for the last 24 hours. As soon as I started trying to find a new apartment, he only showed remorse. We were still living together, and he was going out of his way to be polite, and thoughtful and give me the space I had asked for.

It was really difficult to find an apartment I could afford without a roommate, and it was even more difficult to find a roommate.

I didn't have a support system there. So, after a couple of weeks, I stopped looking for a new place, and we got back together.

He clearly had a substance abuse problem but wasn't always drunk. Although we didn't see each other much that first year of our relationship, he wasn't getting out of control drunk on our one day off work together. He could have been getting drunk every night while I was at work, but I didn't see it. Nearly every night when I came home, he was already in bed asleep. I saw some evidence that he might be abusing his prescription drugs, but I didn't have any experience with people using drugs other than alcohol and weed. I didn't really know what signs to look for.

I lived on the completely opposite side of the country from pretty much everyone I knew. I had a few good work friends, but I didn't feel close enough to any of them to talk about much of my personal life, especially the upsetting parts. A few of my trail crew friends also decided to stay in Alaska after our AmeriCorps service ended, but my boyfriend thought they were superficial and not good friends. I didn't really believe that the people I had grown so close to over my first six months in Alaska didn't care about me.

I guess it was easier to let them slowly drift away than to keep having arguments with my boyfriend about hanging out with them.

By the time we got engaged, about 11 months into our relationship, he was the only person I socialized with besides brief interactions with my coworkers while at work and weekly video calls with my family. About a year after we met, my boyfriend and I moved to another state so I could establish residency and be eligible for in-state tuition before applying for graduate school.

I only applied to one school. If I hadn't gotten in the first time, I would talk to the faculty, find out what I needed to do to get accepted, and then reapply. This was my dream. At first, my boyfriend was on board. I had already gotten a job in the new state before we moved, and he was going to look for work when we got there.

Once we got there, he decided it was too hard for him to find new work, so he cashed out his small retirement fund to live on for a few months. We were planning to get married that year. As our wedding day approached, I felt hesitant and anxious, like something wasn't right.

I didn't voice these concerns out loud because I didn't have anyone to tell. I grew up learning that following the rules is what keeps you safe. It sounds ridiculous to me now, but I felt like I had to marry him since I'd told him I would. If you tell someone you're going to do something, you follow through and do it. Those are the rules.

Plus, you're supposed to get married. You like someone, date them for a while, get married, and then have kids. You don't have to like them all the time; you just have to make sure you seem happy from the outside. That's just what you do.

My boyfriend had been isolating me almost from day one of our relationship, but it was difficult for me to see or realize. It was easy to explain away. I'm naturally an introvert, and it's normal for me to only have a few close relationships at one time. It takes me a while to make friends.

I was only in Alaska for a year and a half, and then we moved to another new state where I also didn't know anyone. I guess I thought it would get better. Yeah, sure, there were a few people I'd started hanging out with who he didn't really like, but at some point, I'd meet some friends he liked.

Looking back now, I can see that he isolated me on purpose so it would be easier to control me; and it worked. Maybe if I had felt close enough to someone to talk about my doubts, I wouldn't have married him. Maybe if I had been able to tell anyone about our relationship, they would have noticed red flags that I couldn't see, and maybe they wouldn't have let me explain them away.

Once we got married, everything got worse and more intense. This was when my husband started abusing me in ways that I actually recognized as abuse, but it was already too late. I was already trapped. He controlled me, and since we had now legally entwined our lives by getting married, he had even more power over me.

There were no physical shackles, but he was in my mind. He kept me on edge almost all the time. There was no safe place for me to relax and let down my guard, not even in my own head. He was gaslighting me, blaming me for everything, and using all the vulnerable things I had ever shared with him to embarrass and shame me.

He remained unemployed while I worked a full-time job just above minimum wage. We had to apply for food stamps to make ends meet.

When I went grocery shopping, I'd go into the store with a list of dollar amounts available on the food stamp card, our debit card, and a credit card.

I would be at the grocery store with the calculator on my phone, adding things up as I shopped, including weighing the bulk items to calculate an exact price. I had to know exactly how much money I had available on each card because if I went over on one, all the cashier would see was that I had an insufficient balance.

On a regular grocery shopping trip, I would be splitting the total amount between two or three cards. My husband was contributing nothing to our finances and getting angry at me almost every day for "hoarding money," aka, paying our bills, keeping the car running so I could get to my job, and buying groceries.

About a year after we got married, I quit my job to start graduate school full-time. That's when my husband finally found a job. When he was the one making the money, he became even more controlling about the finances and over me. Around this time, he progressed from alcohol and weed and started to get into street drugs. At first, I didn't know what was happening.

He started acting really odd, sometimes staying up for days and not really being all with it. He started working an overnight job. I later found out he'd sometimes skip work and go out all night to get high. It was a very quick progression from me noticing something was off to him being high, or coming down from being high, almost all the time. I tried to help but didn't know how, and he didn't want my help. He got more violent and unpredictable as he used drugs more and more. I did my best to stay on track with school and avoid him when he was too high.

I made some friends at my job and later in school. Yet my husband always found ways to stop those relationships from forming before they got too deep. He would call out and focus on a person's character flaws, usually made up but with just enough basis, in reality, to seem plausible. Then he would hound me about it.

He would insult my character for hanging out with people like that until I just stopped hanging out with them. Or he'd get drunk and act wildly inappropriate in front of them, so they didn't want to see us again, or I was too embarrassed to see them again. I was able to hang on to some long-distance friendships.

These friends were far enough away that he didn't see them as a threat as long as they didn't take too much of my focus.

The summer between my two years of graduate school, I went back to where I grew up for a wedding. My husband knew it would raise eyebrows if I didn't show up at some important family events. Therefore, he was okay with me going even though he didn't come with me. Initially, my husband was charming with my family, and then he tended to limit his time with them.

They'd come to visit, and he'd be around for a day or two on his best behavior and then make himself scarce. He'd go on some family vacations with us, but often he'd come up with last-minute excuses to explain why he couldn't go, and I should just go without him. When he did visit with my family, he somehow made it my job to keep him from doing anything that would ruin his reputation with my family. I spent most of my time trying to keep the things I knew would make my family uncomfortable out of sight, but that was an impossible task.

My husband charmed some of the people in my family in the same ways he charmed me, and they explained away behaviors that were inconsistent with his charming persona, just like I did.

Other people in my family pretended not to see what was happening because it made them uncomfortable. They looked the other way and didn't want to know more. They blamed me for bringing my husband into the family as if I had made a decision to get trapped in an abusive marriage. There was a real "you made your bed, now lie in it" vibe.

When I got home from the wedding, my husband picked me up at the airport. He called because he couldn't find me. He was so high that he couldn't even figure out where he was. I found him eventually, and I drove us home. The apartment was a disaster. He'd filled up the trash, and instead of taking it out, he just found a big cardboard box he could fill with more trash. He didn't even line it with a trash bag. It was soggy and smelly.

There was stuff everywhere. It was like he had taken out everything he owned and just strewn it around the apartment. Our bed was covered in random stuff, like books, a wrench, and a plate. I remember pushing stuff out of the way to sit down on the bed and just cry. I had a break from this misery for a week, and it was painful to return to it.

By the time I got to my second year of graduate school, I was in constant survival mode.

Not once in our entire relationship did my abuser hit me or put his hands on me in a violent way. If there's one thing you take away from this story, please know that domestic abuse is about power and control.

Physical violence is one way abusers punish and control their victims, but the root of domestic abuse is coercive control. Each abuser tailors their tactics to their specific victim's worst fears and deepest insecurities. For me, coercive control looked like marathon psychological torture sessions. There was a constant need to stay alert to any changes in mood or hints of what might happen next. The drugs made him more unpredictable and scarier, but they didn't make him abuse me.

For hours on end, he would constantly keep me unsettled. He'd keep me from sleeping. He'd come into the room I was in and do something disruptive. He would turn the light on or off, take my computer while I was working on it, or just start taking random stuff. I knew from experience that if he took stuff, he was either going to lock it up so I couldn't get to it or throw it away.

Nothing physically stopped me from taking the stuff right back out of the trash if he threw it away.

But I knew he would explode with rage and just start breaking things if I did take them out of the trash. If I kept my cool and pretended not to be upset at all, he would escalate to more dangerous things, like locking up my keys and wallet so I couldn't leave or conspicuously cleaning his guns in front of me.

If I tried to keep him out by locking the door to the room I was in, he would literally just break down the door. Then, he would burst into the room with a sick, twisted smile on his face and pretend he had just walked in through the door like normal. Or he'd change out the doorknob while I wasn't home so the door wouldn't lock anymore.

If I tried to barricade myself in the room, he'd just push right through and come in, making a nonchalant comment about how it was weird that there was something in the way of the door. He was trying to break me, forcing me to act as though I believed he wasn't abusing me, even as he was torturing me. I could leave to go to school. But if I was gone too long, I might come home to find trash dumped on the floor, plastic melted on the stovetop, or something I liked destroyed.

He saw my education as his ticket to a more comfortable life.

I'd get a well-paying job, and he'd be able to live more comfortably. He designed his torture to keep me always guessing. To push me to my limits, but not to completely destroy me because I still had to graduate if I was going to be his life-long free ride.

He wanted me to make more money he could live off of but felt emasculated by me being the more educated one with more earning potential. Therefore, he withheld sex as a punishment. But the way he did it was to shame me and blame me for not being good enough at sex. He said my body was dysfunctional for not being able to orgasm when and how he wanted it to. It all boiled down to him saying that I wasn't even worth his time to have sex with.

There was no winning, just surviving. If I didn't react at all, he'd escalate things. If I let on that I was really terrified or really cared about something, he would also escalate things. I was constantly working to show him just the right amount of a reaction so he could get his sadistic fix of pleasure from torturing me and then leave me alone with the minimum amount of destruction. I was spending all of my energy and wits on staying alive, staying as safe as I could, and getting my master's degree simultaneously.

I had no time to think about how bad this was or if I had other options.

One day he was high, screaming at me, and smashing drinking glasses. Even though he was stumbling and staggering, he decided he was going to leave in the car. I begged him not to drive. He took off in the car anyway, and I was sure he was going to kill someone or himself driving that intoxicated, so I called the police. He didn't even have a valid license at that point. He was high, and he had taken **MY** car.

This was the first time I had ever called the police on him, and I immediately learned that the police were not going to help me. The police first made sure I knew that since we were married, it didn't matter if the car was only in my name; my husband had every right to it. They seemed unconcerned about the fact that he was driving high and without a license. Finally, they called him, and he said he was parked somewhere safe now, so the police shrugged and said, "nothing else we can do." They just listened to him on the phone and took his word for it.

The police did, however, interrogate *me*. When they found out I felt unsafe because of the guns my husband kept in the house, they made me voluntarily surrender the guns.

By voluntarily, I mean, technically, I guess I had a choice, but the police officers made it seem like there was no other option and that I had to do this. They literally rolled their eyes at me when I told them that one of the guns was in my name because my husband had made me go to a gun show and take the background check to purchase it. The way those police officers treated me was condescending and patronizing.

They made me feel like this was all my fault. They said I could just tell my husband the police took the guns and that I had no choice. But an important thing they didn't tell me is that when your abuser wants the guns back, he'll be able to call the police department and find out that you were the one who put your name on that form to voluntarily surrender his guns.

Since I was the one who surrendered them, I was the only one who was legally allowed to pick them up from the police. After a certain number of days or weeks, your property becomes the police department's property if you don't pick it up. So once my abuser knew all this, he ramped up his abuse as the deadline for reclaiming the guns approached. I eventually had to pick them up and bring them home to my angry abuser.

That night he left driving high; he ended up staying away for a couple of days. During this time, he stopped by the bank and took my name off of our shared checking account. I didn't get a notice. I didn't have to give permission. He just took away my access to our money.

He later told me that since he was staying away to cool down from being upset at me, it was the least I could do to make sure he had enough money to stay at a hotel. That he was worried I'd drain the bank account, so he was just protecting himself. I was able to set up a student checking account with my university, so at least I had a safer place to put money.

My parents came to visit me, so I got away from home for a week. While I was away, though, my husband started apologizing to me. He admitted his drug use had gotten out of control and said he would get help.

When I found out that he had been injecting street drugs and having unprotected sex with strangers, I felt numb. I knew he had been lying to me for months, but by the time he finally confessed the truth, he had exhausted me so much that all I felt was numb. That's probably the first time I thought to myself, "I think I should be more upset by this. It's weird that I'm not more upset about this."

He made public apologies on social media and told everyone he was struggling with addiction and going to get help. A few days after I agreed to stay with him, his drug use got out of control again. I was still paying all of our bills, and he was spending his paychecks on drugs.

As his drug use got worse, he quit his job before he got fired or just got fired and told me he quit. He started locking me out of the apartment randomly and keeping stuff I needed for school, like the bicycle I used to get to campus, textbooks, notes from class, and my laptop, locked inside with him. He started leaving randomly for hours or days at a time. Sometimes he wouldn't take keys at all, and sometimes he'd take both his keys and mine.

If he didn't take the keys, I'd have to leave the door unlocked until he came home. Otherwise, he would throw a loud, messy, public fit about me locking him out. It would be way worse if I wasn't home at the time. I worried about a stranger breaking in whether I was home or not. At least I could leave if I had to and take my keys, so I'd know I'd be able to get back in. When he took both sets of keys, I couldn't leave. I was sure he would lock me out and make me suffer if I wasn't home when he got home.

I didn't even want to go hang out in the yard for fear I wouldn't see him get home, and he'd lock me out. Sometimes he'd come home looking like he'd been tromping through the woods for days. He'd have sticks in his hair and blackberry thorns in his feet. At some point in the middle of my last semester of graduate school, he scared himself into seeking out rehab. I'm not sure what happened, but one night he said he was scared and needed help. He asked me to take him to the emergency room right away, and I did.

The emergency room visit led to him getting a bed at a hospital for a few days to detox. They got him on the waiting list for a rehab facility and then sent him home to wait for a few weeks until a spot opened up. The first week home, he started using again. Then as my graduation approached, he sobered up for a couple of weeks, and things seemed hopeful again. I straggled across the finish line, dropping off my last overdue assignment at my professor's office on my way to the graduation ceremony. But I did it (thanks to a couple of very generous and understanding professors).

Shortly after I graduated, when my husband was on the third or fourth week of waiting for a spot in rehab, he started drinking again and quickly got back into street drugs.

When a spot opened up, he did go to rehab, but he was only there a couple of weeks before he started buying drugs from other rehab patients and wouldn't commit to staying sober, so they kicked him out. He told me he didn't want to be in rehab while I was struggling to pay the bills and looking for a job. He said he could work temporary jobs to make us some money.

In the couple of weeks he'd been in rehab, and I'd been at home without his constant chaos, I had applied for dozens of jobs. As the summer progressed and I started getting call-backs for job interviews, mostly out of state, he became increasingly controlling. I had to sell my car to pay rent for what I hoped would only be a couple of months until I could get a real job.

I had found an online gig writing copy, so I had some money trickling in to buy food. During this time, my abuser constantly berated me about selling the car and "hoarding the money." He said he was working temporary jobs but was mostly out getting high. I didn't see any money from him to help with the bills.

One night, he was high and scary; I just needed to get away from him. I was going to ride my bicycle to a nearby motel. He got a knife and stabbed my bike tire to try to stop me from leaving.

He called one of my family members, who lived in a different time zone, where it was way later. He woke my family member up in the middle of the night, claiming it was an emergency and that he needed help. He lied and said I was drunk, and he was just trying to stop me from riding my bike drunk. He asked my family member to help convince me not to leave.

He was trying to use my family to play a part in controlling me. I called a cab. The cab showed up, and my abuser came running out of the apartment, yelling at the cab driver. I got in and told the driver to go. My abuser got to the open passenger side window and asked to see the taxi driver's credentials. I had to repeat a few times that I was the one paying for a ride and to just go before the driver finally stopped listening to my abuser and drove away.

I could only afford to stay away at a hotel for a couple of nights, so I went back home. We were barreling towards homelessness or moving for a new job, whichever came first. I didn't have a plan other than I had paid up the rent through the end of August. I had my fingers crossed I would get one of those jobs I'd interviewed for before I ran out of money.

I started packing up, knowing that either way, we'd have to get out of that apartment by the end of the summer. My abuser became paranoid and thought I secretly planned to move away without him. I wish that's what I was doing. I was still under his control and had kind of lost hope that anyone would ever do anything to stop him from hurting me.

When I finally got a job halfway across the country, he suddenly became much, much nicer. He cut way down on his drug use. He started helping with the packing. He said he was committed to doing better and would get help when we moved.

When we moved, he did start going to mental health care services regularly. Then he started abusing his medications, not following the prescriptions and taking them in ways that got him high. He said he would start going to AA meetings again and thought we should get a puppy so he'd have a routine and purpose. In hindsight, getting a puppy at that moment in our lives was ridiculous, but I went along with it, and in the end, the puppy saved my life.

One day, I had set up a chair against the door and was sitting in it so he couldn't get in. I just wanted some peace, a moment by myself to watch a show, but he wouldn't let me.

He kept banging and pushing on the door. I had to push back to keep him from getting in. I was actively resisting, so he called the police on me. He told them I had locked myself in a room and he was worried about me.

My abuser let the police officers into the apartment. They told me I had to come out of the room because they needed to make sure I was okay. They separated us. One talked to my abuser and the other to me, but we were still only about 10 feet apart.

My abuser was playing the confused but caring husband. He didn't know why I would lock myself in a room and was just concerned about me. The one thing I will say for the police officers is that they clearly did not believe my abuser's act.

I just wanted them to leave. I knew they weren't going to help me. I was reluctant to say anything, especially with my abuser standing so nearby, but the police officer kept pushing me for details. Finally, I realized that the police suspected that some abuse was going on, and they were not going to drop it, so the quickest way to get them to leave was to tell them what they wanted to hear.

In a whisper, while the other police officer was engaging my abuser in conversation across the room, I told the police officer that my husband was high almost all the time on his prescription medications. I told him that he tormented me, deprived me of sleep, and made me feel unsafe by cleaning and playing with his guns in the house.

Did he hit you?

No.

Did he try to strangle you?

No.

Did he point a gun at you?

No.

Did he tell you he was going to kill you?

No.

The police officer asked me a few more details, like if there were any illegal drugs or paraphernalia in the house that I knew of (no) and what kind of gun my husband had (a rifle). "Well," they said, "there's nothing we can do. There's nothing we can arrest him on. He doesn't need a permit for a rifle.

You should tell his doctor about that prescription abuse, though. Here, take this." The cop handed me a little blue half sheet of paper with domestic abuse hotlines on it. Gee, thanks; I am really glad that two gruff strangers with guns showed up to force all this out of me so they could give me a piece of paper that if my abuser sees, he'll probably get upset about.

Who, exactly, are the police here to protect? My abuser knew he wouldn't get in trouble. He was so smug about this incident that he started using it as a joke and a threat, "Hey, don't do that, or I'll have to call the cops on you."

About three weeks after my abuser called the cops on me, we got our puppy. We had planned to adopt her for months and were just waiting for her to get old enough. Maybe if everything hadn't already been arranged ahead of time, I would have backed out, but you know what, puppies are really cute, and it was something I was excited about.

We named her Siena after a medieval city in Italy. We had been there on vacation a few years prior. That was before we got married and when the abuse was still pretty invisible to me.

I remembered sitting with my boyfriend in the sun on the city's brick plaza, watching people at cafes, or having little picnics. It was a really nice memory.

At first, my abuser was attentive to Siena. I think, for a moment, he imagined a different life was possible for himself. A life where he wasn't in pain all the time and could actually open his heart to this adorable little puppy, or maybe he was just manipulating me.

After a few weeks, I was doing all the puppy care. Midnight pee breaks, early morning pee breaks, going to work, and coming home on my lunch break to take her for a mid-day walk. Siena would wake me up at 5 am every morning, and I'd take her out for a little walk. Then, I'd go back inside and make myself some coffee.

My abuser was usually still asleep at this time, so I had an hour or two of solitude before I had to go to work. I'd lounge on the couch with Siena curled up on my chest and stomach while I drank my coffee and watched it get light outside. She snuggled her way into my heart.

In my abuser's mind, the only legit reasons I had to leave the apartment were for the annoying things he didn't want to do, like working, grocery shopping, and walking the dog.

Occasional family and social functions were also okay to maintain a public façade of normalcy. He didn't need to be physical with me to control me. So as long as it didn't seem like I was getting too close to anyone, it helped shield him from suspicion.

Because I was out walking the puppy in my neighborhood so often, I kept running into this person who brought their dog to a neighborhood park to play fetch. Other dog people can't resist saying hello when you have an itsy-bitsy adorable puppy. That spring, we formed a friendship by hanging out with our dogs at the park. It was the only relationship I had outside of the coworkers I'd gotten to know since moving for my job.

I don't know exactly what happened every day when I was at work and my abuser was home alone with Siena, but I caught glimpses of it sometimes. One day I got home from work, and my abuser was outside building a snowman. He had Siena outside with him on a tie-out, and she was whimpering and whining. I didn't know how long he'd had her outside, but she was a little 15lb puppy, and she was shivering.

My abuser acted as though he couldn't hear or see her distress. I immediately took her inside and warmed her up.

I realized he did the same thing to me, pretending he couldn't hear or see my distress. After years of being trapped and having every tentative step towards getting help squashed, I had learned to endure.

Experience had shown me that the law wouldn't protect me, and the police wouldn't protect me. Getting married had taken away my individual rights by legally binding me to someone who wanted to control me. By this point, I had resigned myself to struggling and surviving, but realizing that my abuser was hurting Siena was the motivation I needed. Maybe no one would help me, but I could help my puppy.

One night, I made an impulse decision to get the heck out of there; for a few hours at least. I told my friend, the person I had met at the park, that my husband was getting on my nerves and I needed a break. I asked if I could come over and hang out for a while. They weren't going to be home that evening but said their roommate would be fine with me hanging out and watching TV at their place.

As I walked out the door, I casually told my abuser I was going to hang out with a friend for a while. I knew he'd be upset, but I didn't care. He followed me outside and yelled at me from our front porch as I walked away.

He knew I was coming back because I didn't take Siena. He knew I'd come back to take care of her, but it still pissed him off. It was reckless and could have ended terribly, but it was also the first step I took towards freedom, towards defiance.

I went over to my friend's place, and their roommate was drunk. Considering what I normally lived around, it didn't make me think twice about staying there. The drunk roommate was actually quite pleasant and friendly. And maybe because they were a drunk stranger and not someone I really knew, that made it easier for me to talk to them. They were the first person I told about what was really going on at home. I stayed on the couch there for the night but then left really early in the morning to go home and take care of Siena.

When I had left abruptly the night before, it sent my abuser into a tailspin. Immediately upon entering the apartment, I understood that the situation was more volatile and dangerous now. I don't think he was expecting me to leave like that; I had caught him off guard. He was ramping up his tactics because he perceived a threat. Was *I* the threat? If I was the threat, that meant I had some power over him.

He was methodically moving things from all over the apartment into our bedroom. He had screwed a piece of wood into the bedroom door and frame so that when he wasn't in there with the door locked, he could secure the room by screwing the door shut from the outside. Every time he left the room to get more stuff, he screwed the door shut and walked around with the drill in his hand.

It was ominous and threatening. Not because he was locking stuff in the room, but because I imagined the next time I wanted to avoid him, maybe instead of breaking down the door, he'd decide it was easier to torture me by screwing the door shut from the outside and keeping me captive.

I decided not to show him I was afraid and just pretended everything was fine. I made myself some coffee, took Siena for a walk, and sat down on the couch for my morning puppy snuggles. I heard the sound of the drill going intermittently in the background. Being honest to someone else the night before had made me realize I had to do something, but I wasn't sure where to begin. I still was thinking more about getting Siena to safety than myself. In fact, a lot of what I had shared the night before was about how my abuser treated Siena.

I didn't have a plan at this point but thinking about leaving had made me hopeful for the first time in a long time. While I was sitting there, at a loss for how to take action, the friendly roommate messaged. They had talked with my friend. They had explained the seriousness of my situation, and they had both agreed I could come stay on their couch and bring Siena with me. A person I barely knew did what the police and the legal system would not do for me. The friendly roommate validated my experience and offered me help.

I let that offer sink into my body for a few moments. It felt scary but hopeful. It was the lifeline I needed at exactly the moment I was ready to grab onto it. I didn't plan my escape at all; I seized an opportunity. I got up off the couch and grabbed a backpack.

At this point, I had a lot of my clothes and things in one of our spare rooms because I was never sure if I would have access to our bedroom. Even before my husband screwed the door shut, he had a habit of locking me out of the bedroom. My body was shaking, and my brain was in overdrive.

I grabbed clothing at random, my brain trying to send me helpful coherent thoughts like, enough shirts, make sure you get pants too.

My abuser walked in, looked at me, and then left without saying anything. He came back a minute later and, still silent, grabbed my laptop and then started pouring water into my backpack.

He stared at me, daring me to stop him. His eyes were empty. I guess I hadn't looked him in the eye in a long time and was shocked by what I saw. Was there even anyone human in there anymore?

I hurried downstairs while he was busy using the drill to open the bedroom door so he could stash my laptop. I thought if I was quick enough, I might be able to get Siena on her leash and get out before he realized I was gone. But, no, he came running in, saw Siena's leash in my hand, and grabbed her. He took her upstairs, and I heard the drill going. He was locking her in the bedroom.

My body was screaming at me to leave, but my brain wouldn't let me. I didn't completely freeze, but I was stuck, pacing back and forth in the same spot again and again. Walking a few feet towards the door, turning around to go towards the puppy, then back towards the door, towards the puppy, then again towards the door. It was involuntary. My brain was panicking; there were no real coherent thoughts. Door, puppy, door, puppy, door, puppy!

I don't know how long I did that for, but suddenly I saw a puppy trotting towards me. I don't know what happened upstairs. I don't know how she got out of the bedroom, but I grabbed her, an open bag of her food that was nearby, and ran.

I ran through the neighborhood, carrying a 30lb bag of dog food, with a puppy trotting beside me. First, I got to the nearest intersection and looked back to make sure he wasn't following me before turning the corner, out of sight. A few blocks away from home, Siena stopped short and demanded a bathroom break. That's the only time in my life that I have not picked up my dog's poop, and I still felt bad about it even though I was literally in the middle of running for my life. I shouted an apology out loud to no one, and we kept running.

I made it to my friend's apartment building shaking and out of breath. I was fumbling around in my backpack for my phone to let them know I was there and needed to be let into the building. But my hands wouldn't work. Fortunately, someone who lived there showed up at that moment and let me in. Right away, my friends found most of my stuff listed for sale on craigslist by my abuser; he'd started listing it the night before.

At this point, I had no belief that the police would help me, but my friends thought it would be worth at least checking if the police could escort me back to the apartment to get some of my stuff. I called the police to explain the situation, and they said they could escort me into the apartment to make sure I was safe.

The police said they didn't get involved in domestic disputes. So, if my abuser said I couldn't take something, they wouldn't let me take it from the apartment. I knew he'd say I couldn't have anything, so going back was pointless.

My friends also encouraged me to call a local domestic abuse hotline to get some guidance on what to do next and find out what resources were available to me. The people on the hotline first made sure I had a safe place to stay, which I did. Then they advised me against getting a restraining order. They told me I should make an appointment with one of their housing advocates to talk about my options for long-term housing.

I made multiple appointments with their housing advocates. When I showed up for the appointments, the advocates weren't there. I'm really glad I happened to have an appointment with my therapist that week.

I felt like I had finally done the really big thing of leaving, but everything was harder now. I thought it was supposed to be better, easier. My therapist gave me a good pep talk and told me how amazing I was for having the courage to leave. They also gave me a few different resources to look into. It ultimately led to me getting some help and being able to get a restraining order against my abuser.

Meanwhile, my phone was blowing up with calls and texts from my abuser. I sent one text that said I didn't want to talk to him and ignored the rest. He was all over the place with his messages. Some were threatening, some were apologetic, and some were meant to make me feel guilty. I think he was just trying everything he could think of to see if anything would get a reaction out of me. He was floundering because I refused to play his games.

A couple of days after I had the appointment with my therapist, the restraining order was granted. I was pretty sure that once the sheriff started knocking on the door to serve the restraining order, my abuser would decide it was time to get out of Dodge. I was grateful that my friends had let me stay with them for the past week, but it was kind of chaotic.

It was a big open apartment with little privacy. There was a lot of drinking and people hanging out way past my bedtime. I believed it was only a matter of days before I could go back to my home. So, I asked a coworker if I could stay with them for a few days at their much calmer, much quieter home, and they agreed.

As I was leaving work that day, I felt like I finally might have control of my life again. And I'm not even kidding you; it started to downpour. I laughed and cried at the same time in relief and joy. I held my arms out, tilted my face toward the sky, and let the rain wash over me. It was the most cliche Shawshank Redemption moment ever. I felt like it was time to let go of the past and start planning for the future, but after a couple of hopeful days, I realized the fight wasn't over.

Trying to navigate temporary places to stay with a puppy was very difficult. I'm glad I had friends who were okay with me bringing a barely potty-trained puppy to their apartments, but each time I asked for help, I had to reveal the truth that I'd been hiding for years. Sure, I knew some people who would have offered to take care of Siena if they had known what was going on. But because of my abuser, I wasn't close enough to anyone to get help with no questions asked.

Because I'd been hiding the truth from everyone for so long, each time I had to tell, it felt like an ordeal. Worrying about a place for Siena to stay limited my options and drove me to get back into my old apartment without knowing for sure it was safe.

If I had known Siena would have a safe place to stay without me having to reveal to more of my acquaintances the utter mess my life was, I would have explored more temporary housing options.

When I fled my abuser, I could have broken my lease using a state domestic violence provision that would have allowed me to walk away. It would have also meant walking away from any claim to my stuff that was still in the apartment, the security deposit, and from having a place to live.

I could afford rent at the apartment I already had, but I couldn't afford a security deposit equal to a month's rent, plus the first month's rent, and depending on the landlord, possibly last month's rent as well. I couldn't swing two to three months' rent upfront to get a new apartment.

So, I went to my property management company's office in person to explain the situation. I gave them a copy of the restraining order that was approved by a judge.

The order said my abuser wasn't allowed to be at or near the apartment. I wanted them to change the locks. The management company told me that *I* would have to get the man I had a restraining order against to sign a form relinquishing his rights to the lease.

When I told them that having a restraining order against my abuser also meant that I wasn't supposed to contact him, they just repeated that the only way they could change the locks was if he signed the form. I couldn't afford to move. I felt like I had no choice but to stay there. I couldn't even get a $20 security measure put in place that would make me feel a little safer.

My abuser didn't answer the door for the sheriff to serve him the restraining order. He kept texting and leaving me voicemails asking what the sheriff wanted. Then he switched to saying he was going to leave and just needed some money. I ignored it all, and technically he wasn't violating the restraining order because he hadn't been served yet. I knew he didn't know anyone in the state or even the region of the country where we lived.

Reading between the lines of his threats and demands for money from me, and with some friends keeping track of his social media, I eventually had reasonable proof that he was halfway across the country. I didn't plan for safety, and I got lucky. I needed a place to live, and it was clear from my experiences that it would be up to me to figure this out.

One morning before work, I went back to my apartment. My abuser was gone. But he'd sold or stolen anything that had monetary value. He'd destroyed or thrown away everything else. Walking through the apartment that first day back, and over the next few weeks and months, I slowly cleaned everything up. That is when I started to see that this man was unraveling.

He was unhinged and still dangerous to me, but I started to see the cracks. I began to see him as less terrifying and more human. What used to cause me terror now seemed desperately sad and absurd. He had left me ransom notes scrawled on torn pieces of cardboard or broken pieces of furniture. He demanded ridiculous amounts of money that we both knew I didn't have for him to return items that had sentimental value to me.

He also made sure to leave several nasty messages about what a bitch I was on different items in permanent marker or by carving the words into their surfaces. He left several notes that seemed more positive but were outright lies. In one, he claimed that even though our relationship was ending, the silver lining was that I had made it through graduate school, "I'm so proud of you," he wrote, "The best thing I ever helped with."

I guess he was just trying to cover all his bases, some threats, some insults, some gaslighting. He left tubs of dirty dishes filled with water and rotting food. He carved up the walls with knives. He smudged bright colored paints on light fixtures and walls. He ripped shelves out of the walls leaving holes. He smashed and tore up dishes, books, papers, photographs, clothing, jewelry, art, blankets, and furniture.

He peed everywhere, in every single room, on every single thing he had strewn across the floors of the apartment. We had a two-story, three-bedroom apartment. He took what I can only assume must have been days to systematically go through and pee on everything in every room.

At first, it felt shocking and terrifying that someone could have that much cruelty and bitterness inside and that he was directing at me with such dedication and meticulous attention. As I've told my story more, and now that I'm safe, I can't help laughing at it. He was still living there at the time, and when I imagine him chugging water and stewing in his own urine-drenched vengeance for days, that's just so absurd that it makes me laugh.

My brain couldn't really process the loss of 95% of my material possessions. Over the next several months, I was constantly caught off guard with sudden realizations that I didn't have those things anymore. About two months after I got back into my apartment, I was planning to plant vegetable seeds at my community garden plot. I was packing up some tools and gardening gloves and was getting ready to head out when I suddenly realized I didn't have any seeds to plant.

The seeds, which I'd bought months before I left my abuser, weren't something I had found while cleaning up the trashed apartment. So, my brain just assumed I had them somewhere, right up until the moment I needed them.

Nearly two years after I left him, I randomly found some of the items he had written me ransom notes for hidden in the basement, stuffed inside the walls, and hidden out of sight on the rafters.

I don't really think he ever intended to tell me where they were, even if I had sent him the exorbitant ransom he had asked for. I truly think he enjoyed the idea that they were hidden in the walls of the home I lived in and would always be just beyond my grasp. There's probably still some of my stuff hidden in the walls of that apartment.

Almost as soon as I fled my abuser, I called Legal Aid, but I made a little too much money to qualify for their services. I found a lawyer who specialized in domestic abuse cases through my employee assistance program. I would have had no idea how to find a lawyer on my own, let alone one who had the right experience to help me.

I didn't know what a retainer was when I had my consultation with the lawyer. My heart sank when she told me I'd need a few thousand dollars upfront before she could even start working on my case. The only reason I was able to hire a lawyer for the divorce was because my family gave me enough money to pay the retainer upfront.

My abuser made the divorce difficult by actively avoiding participating in the process. He wouldn't give an address to my lawyer, and he kept moving. It took more time than it should have and cost more money to prove he had been legally notified at each step in the process. Several months after I got divorced, I still had a long road ahead of me to completely pay off all the debts and damage to my credit score my abuser had caused. However, a few months of paychecks without someone coercing money out of me had put me in a much more stable financial situation.

During this time, I reconnected with my best friend from middle school, who was living in Japan. I shopped for deals on flights, and because my friend offered me a free place to stay, I was able to afford a trip to Japan. My friend could speak a little Japanese, but I didn't speak any. I had never even imagined going to that part of the world, but this was an opportunity for an adventure. We hadn't seen each other in years, but we just picked up where we left off.

My friend is a foodie, so they took me to the best places to eat. I made a deal with myself that I was going to try everything they ordered us. A couple of times, I took a bite and decided that food was not for me.

But I tried them all, and I discovered a bunch of new foods that I loved.

After years of being guarded, I felt safe enough to let my guard down and had a fantastic adventure. There was something powerful about reconnecting positively with someone who knew me when I was a kid. It helped me remember who I used to be.

Shortly after that trip, I adopted a second dog. I named her Mei (pronounced like "may") after the Meiji Shrine I had visited with my friend in Japan. When I announced I was getting a second dog, a family member told me I just needed a boyfriend.

They were trying to shame me into acting "normal." I loved my glorious single dog mom life. I wasn't ashamed or embarrassed to want two dogs and no boyfriend. For most of my life, I had been conditioned to conform to what other people wanted in order to survive and avoid punishment. I rarely believed that there was anything wrong with me. I just knew it was easier and safer to be what other people wanted or expected me to be.

When I started embracing and nourishing who I was, I was delightfully surprised at just how silly I could be and how much joy it brought me to do things because they made me giggle.

So, I made one of those cutesy pregnancy announcement photos with my feet, Siena's paws, and a set of empty dog boots between us to formally announce the upcoming adoption of my second dog.

When I fled my abuser, something shifted permanently inside me. It was a complete upheaval; my foundation was rocked. My whole sense of self crumbled apart. It forced me to take stock of myself for maybe the first time ever. I noticed some parts of myself that didn't serve me anymore, so I let go of them.

I discovered some long-neglected parts that needed to be nourished. I had to build some new parts too. Parts that better suited who I had become. I changed, but not everyone I knew changed with me. It didn't happen right away, but some time after I fled my abuser, I realized I needed more space from some of the people who knew me before and during the abuse, including my family. I took a big step back from those relationships for a little while.

I didn't make an announcement; I just stopped initiating contact. Some of them kept reaching out to me while others didn't. I let my calls go to voicemail unless we had planned it ahead of time. I allowed myself time and space to consider how or if I wanted to respond to voicemails and texts.

I also didn't date for a couple of years because I needed time for myself.

It's kind of like when you turn down the volume, so the music isn't drowning everything out. Maybe you still leave it on quietly in the background, but it's not the focus anymore. I had turned down the volume on other people to focus on myself. But I found that I was empty and silent. I survived the first three decades of my life because I adapted and shaped myself to fit in the spaces and roles that others wanted me to fill.

The parts of me that had survived to this point had only survived because they learned to shrink down, be quiet, and stay out of the way. First, I had to show those parts of me some tenderness and let them know it was safe to come out of hiding. Then, I had to learn how to listen to them. I worked with my therapist a lot to figure this out.

My therapist gave me a list of values and asked me to pick the ones that I connected with; the ones that felt like maybe they were my core values. Then we talked through each one to see how I lived those values. How did my thoughts and actions align with those values?

She drew a chart on a piece of paper while we were talking and had me mark on the paper how important each value was to me on a scale of 1-10. And then, she asked me to think about my abuser and mark on the paper how important each of the values was to him, based on how I had seen him act. Well, shit. I'd never even thought about that before. He and I did not have the same priorities at a deep core level; I had never realized that before.

My therapist had me do this with a couple of my family members. Then they suggested I use the same exercise when getting to know new people. Because I was used to being coerced, to having my boundaries pushed and broken, I found that writing important things down helped me stay true to myself. I could go back to what I had written down to remind myself what I wanted and what was acceptable to me.

After I spent some time understanding who I was, I started to take some cautious steps toward rebuilding some old relationships with my new boundaries in place. I started with the people I felt the safest with and who I felt were open to adjusting the way our relationship looked.

There were stops and starts. I took it slow, both for me and others so that we could get used to the changes. It's not easy to ask someone you've known for a long time to treat you differently than they always have. People broke my boundaries at first, and that's normal. I just had to keep reminding them and sticking to my part of the agreement. If I had told them I would end the conversation if they didn't stick to my boundaries, I followed through, and we tried again another day.

I even grew apart from those who first offered me safety on their couch. They helped save my life, and I will always be grateful for that, but it's natural and okay for relationships to change and even end. That's a part of life. Clinging to the relationship and desperately trying to make it work no matter what is unnatural and unhealthy.

I remember a specific moment when I talked to some family members after a long pause in interacting with them. I found myself in a situation I had experienced with them many times before. As I listened to them bicker this time, I felt like I was floating away from them. The compulsion to play my old role in the family dynamic was, maybe not gone completely, but very faint.

I could shrug my shoulders and turn away. I finally realized that I didn't have to get involved. I had choices.

My mom and I have spent years deconstructing our old relationship and building a new one. We're still working on it, and we probably always will be. But, no matter what happens, I know she loves me and accepts me for who I am without trying to change me. She has proven that to me over and over again. I have a different relationship with my mom than I used to; it's a much better, mutually respectful, and loving relationship. We found what works for us and we're both committed to continuing to work on it.

I also learned to recognize when I was falling into old, unhealthy behavior patterns and how to hold myself accountable with compassion. If that happened, I tried to figure out why.
Was it an unconscious slip into old behaviors because that was how I used to act in that situation or around those people?

What could I do to set myself up to not be in that situation in the future or catch myself and stop that thought pattern? Was this an old survival mechanism kicking in, like putting others' needs in front of mine that had been triggered by something another person had said or done?

Being analytical like that made these complex emotions more accessible to me. It was a way to notice patterns over time and recognize when people were trying to influence or manipulate me.

People showed me who they were. The way they respected (or didn't respect) my boundaries showed me who wanted to have a relationship with me and who just wanted to coerce me back into being the person they used to know so they could go back to using me. I've gone no contact with some people, both temporarily and indefinitely. I don't feel safe with them, and they have shown me over and over again that they want me to be someone they can control.

Before I started dating again, I wrote myself a two-page relationship note that listed things like my dealbreakers in relationships. I wrote what I knew from experience I didn't want in a partner, what I wanted from a romantic relationship, and how I wanted to feel when I was with the person I was dating. I folded it up and kept it in my wallet.

Not every relationship has long-term potential. But if I was starting to feel like it might, I'd check my note as things progressed to see how well the relationship aligned with what I wanted. I also used it in the moment to stop myself from ignoring red flags.

One time, while I was on a date, I pulled it out in the bathroom. I reread the "how do I want to feel around this person" section so that I wouldn't minimize how I was feeling in the moment once I calmed down. I was upset and read my note while I was upset so that I could prove to myself that I did not feel the way I wanted to feel while I was with this person.

My relationship note was a tool that helped me stay true to myself and trust myself again. Below is an excerpt from my relationship note:

<u>*What do I want from a romantic relationship?*</u>

- *companionship*
- *emotional support*
- *friendship*
- *touch*
- *partnership*
- *emotional and intellectual stimulation*
- *travel/adventure/activity partner*
- *independence*
- *encouragement*
- *time/space/support/encouragement to be independent and pursue individual interests*
- *have fun and laugh together*
- *a confidant*

How do I want to feel with this person?

- *understood*
- *supported*
- *joyful*
- *safe*
- *comfortable*
- *safe to be emotionally and physically vulnerable*
- *not judged*
- *happy*
- *safe to make mistakes*
- *loved*
- *wanted*
- *sense of belonging*
- *connectedness*
- *encouraged*
- *cared for*
- *valued*
- *prioritized*
- *trusted*
- *confident*
- *unashamed*

I've been with my current partner for four years now, and I have all the things listed above. Not in a "too good to be true" kind of way, but in a "we built this relationship that works for us over the years with a lot of hard work" kind of way.

Like everyone, we have conflicts to work through, but we do it with a secure, mutually trusting, and respectful foundation in place. I still regularly have moments when I'm struck by a sudden, deep sense of contentment while we're doing something mundane together.

Maybe some part of me didn't believe this would ever be possible. Maybe all the chaos and terror gave me a deeper appreciation of the little moments, like doing the chores with someone who cares about you; Or taking turns voicing the dog's thoughts because it's fun and funny to pretend to include her in your conversations.

Even though I love my partner, I accept the possibility that one or both of us may change in ways that aren't compatible in the future. I feel more secure and committed in this relationship because we don't expect each other to stay the same. I don't feel trapped. This is no rigid "'til death do us part" situation. "Let's do this as long as it's what we both want" is an active commitment to work every day at showing up for each other, creating the space to be honest without being judged, and being willing to adapt to changes while respecting each other and staying true to ourselves.

Because I now invest my energy in people who invest in me in return, everything is easier. Doors have opened that I didn't know existed. People have shown up for me in ways I would never have thought possible. Because I took the time, and keep taking the time, to understand who I am, I can show up as my authentic self. It's okay if I come to a new understanding and change my mind about something.

When I have nothing to hide, my connections with others are more sincere and warm. Because I created safety for myself, I learned that I could let down my guard, at least sometimes.
I'm more resilient and adaptable. Vulnerability isn't a weakness; it's my superpower.

I used to be strong, but I'm not anymore. I was rigid, and other people just kept throwing their baggage on top of my shoulders. I focused all my energy on surviving, being strong, and holding up that weight until I cracked and buckled. In rebuilding, I discovered that I'd rather be resilient than strong.

I became less rigid, less judgmental, and more open-minded when I accepted the discomfort that comes with growing and changing instead of trying to avoid it.

I found myself questioning things I had never thought to question before. Instead of just doing things because I had done them before or because "that's just what people do," I started to ask myself *why* I was doing those things.

One day I told my therapist how someone I knew pretty well, but hadn't seen in a while, had walked past me twice in one week without recognizing me. She looked at me and said, "Kathy, you have changed so much. You even carry yourself differently than you used to. They probably didn't recognize you because you're a different person."

Three years after I fled my abuser, he was shot and killed. He broke into a home, and the homeowner shot him. Since the homeowner was an off-duty law enforcement officer, there was an investigation, and a public report was published about the incident. I read it partially because I wanted to make sure it was true that he was actually dead and could never hurt me again.

The report said he was found smoking a joint on the home's second-story balcony in the middle of the night. When confronted by the homeowner, he said, "You know me, this is my mom's house."

I believe he was so high (on way more drugs than weed) that he really did believe it was his mom's house. He then tried to walk back into the house, and the homeowner kept telling him to stop, but he didn't. They were scared, so they shot him. He died on their bathroom floor before the paramedics arrived.

When I read the report, I mostly felt sad for him. I wondered if he was scared. I wondered if he understood at any time what was actually happening or if he died in a drugged-out stupor. There's a lot of cognitive dissonance with my thoughts about him now and the grief I feel thinking about the violent way his life ended.

The terror I still feel sometimes because of how he treated me. The relief I feel because I know he can never hurt me again. And the freedom his death gave me to live without looking over my shoulder.

I have PTSD. Even with medication and therapy, it affects me every day. My body still tenses up sometimes when I see a stranger who looks like my abuser. One time on a walk, I saw my abuser. He was dead by then, but I saw him standing in front of me. I was walking with someone and having a conversation.

As we walked by this guy, I kept looking at his face, blinking, looking the other way, and then back at him. It was my abuser. But it wasn't because he was dead.

Triggers that remind me of my abuser have gotten less intense and less frequent over time. Maybe after the thousandth time it happens, my body will finally realize that my dead abuser is not coming back to hurt me. As I've worked in therapy to process the trauma from my abusive marriage, I've started to unearth trauma in my body from even farther back in the past.

These days, my most intense triggers are things from my childhood. I froze in a grocery store checkout line because some grumpy customer was yelling at a cashier. I was a little kid again, stuck, being screamed at. I don't even remember checking out. Fifteen minutes later, when I got home, my heart was still racing, and my voice was shaky as I told my partner about what had happened. It's frustrating that triggers like this, things that are part of everyday life, affect me so much. There's no way to avoid them.

Even with PTSD, I'm safe and happy. I have a loving partner, and Mei is literally the sweetest dog in the world. Siena died a couple of years ago, and I miss her.

But I know I gave her the best life I could, and she was happy. I got her safe, and I kept her safe.

My apartment is bright and colorful, and no one ever throws trash on the floor. I've been painting for a couple of years, and as I write this chapter, I'm also finishing up some paintings for an art show. I made myself an artist pseudonym by rearranging some of the letters in my name because it's fun and it makes me giggle.

I've learned that there's no right way to do things, and "I want to be silly" is a great reason to do something. I have lots of houseplants, and tending to them as they grow makes me smile. I have friends and a community.

After getting an official diagnosis of PTSD and getting on medication to help manage my symptoms, I started serving on a local mental health advisory council. I've used my paintings and my story of survival to fundraise for local nonprofits and mutual aid funds that I care about. I can't change what happened to me, but I can do something to stop perpetuating it. My abuser was abused, and he chose to hurt me. I was abused, and I chose to learn how it affected me so I could grow, heal, and contribute positively to my community.

After I got divorced, a lot of intense emotions surfaced. Our wedding anniversary was a few weeks after the divorce was finalized. My therapist suggested that it might be helpful to create some kind of ritual for a tough anniversary like this one. So, I put my engagement ring in my pocket and bicycled along Lake Superior until I found a spot that felt right.

I climbed down some rocks to get off the path and closer to the water. I took the ring out of my pocket and looked at it. Then I looked out to the horizon, where the lake met the sky, and took a deep breath. I took a step back with one foot, so I was in a more powerful throwing stance, and then I launched my engagement ring into the lake.

Physically throwing the last remaining vestige of my marriage into obscurity in the largest freshwater lake in the world was a moment of catharsis and hope. I thought about all I'd survived to get to this point and how I was looking forward to the future for the first time in a long time.

I go back to that spot every year on the wedding anniversary to reflect. In the months leading up to my wedding, I had convinced myself to ignore the feeling that something wasn't right.

I ignored the warning signs, and then I got trapped. Getting free was my second chance at life. Checking in with myself every year is part of how I honor myself. This is how I do something to make sure it never happens to me again. This is how I show myself love.

I sit there, listening to the waves lap against the shore and watching the seagulls on the rocks nearby. I look out at the lake, thinking about how this water travels through the Great Lakes Waterway, through the St. Lawrence River, and out to the Atlantic Ocean. I am not alone; this place and water connect me to the whole world.

I think about what I've struggled with in the last year and what brought me joy. Do my actions and goals still align with my values and desires? It's my time to evaluate if I'm happy with the way I'm living. If I'm not, it's my chance to notice that and do something about it.

Every year when I visit that little rocky beach to commemorate my freedom, I find a piece of beach glass there. I have a jar at home that I put each piece of glass in. It's simply labeled with the date I threw my engagement ring in the lake. There are seven pieces of beach glass in the jar now. Each piece is unique, just like the year of my life it represents.

In that jar, all jumbled together, they represent the life I've built for myself. The jar still has plenty of space to add more beach glass, which both terrifies and delights me. It represents the years to come, the potential for uncertainty and grief, but also for joy and love.

If you or someone you know is experiencing Domestic Violence

National Domestic Violence Hotline
www.thehotline.org
1-800-799-7233

National Sexual Assault Hotline- RAINN
www.rainn.org
1-800-656-4673

Domesticshelters.org

Stand Up Survivor
www.standupsurvivor.org
321-430-5307